THE DISTRO VERSE

How to Build a Distribution Channel That Will Put
You Ahead of 99% of Entrepreneurs

SAVRAJ AURA

In a world as fractured as it is. Where normal is not normal. The tactics taught by someone like me could be your only hope.

Contents

Acknowledgments

I would like to express my heartfelt gratitude to my wife, Erika, the love of my life, whose unwavering support, love, strength, and encouragement have been the foundation of this book. Without you, this project would not have been possible.

I am forever grateful to my wonderful daughters, whose mere presence in my life has sparked the inspiration to embark on this legacy project. Your influence and impact on my journey are immeasurable.

I extend heartfelt gratitude to my remarkable business partners, Tatyana and Samantha. Tatyana's expertise in building my business, crafting offers, and providing insightful frameworks has been invaluable. Samantha's technical prowess and exceptional editing skills have transformed my monumental brain dump into a cohesive and impactful piece of work. Their super-efficiency, brilliant insights, and constant support during the creative process have shaped my business and this book in ways beyond measure. Thank you both for your unwavering commitment and dedication.

I am acutely aware that this book owes its existence to the dedication and collaboration of my worldwide DistroAgents throughout these countless years. Together, we have weathered trials, embraced challenges, celebrated triumphs, and gained invaluable experiences while building businesses and global DistroNetworks from humble beginnings. Your contributions have truly elevated the quality and reach of this book.

I've taken inspiration from many people in the business self-help arena in how they simplify frameworks and concepts to help entrepreneurs at every level. After reading *Dotcom Secrets* by Russell Brunson, I was sold on using doodle art instead of polished corporate illustrations so that you can more easily understand the concepts I'm presenting without them looking boring. Yu-Kai Chou's *Actionable Gamification* was a great help in articulating the ways I motivated my inside sales team and distribution networks over the years. There are countless others, including publications like *The Economist* and *Adweek*. I couldn't possibly name them all here. But what I've learned most was how to teach through storytelling to better articulate what I know. This is the power of taking the time to read other people's work.

I extend my deepest appreciation to everyone mentioned here and to those whose support may not have been acknowledged explicitly. You have all played a significant role in making this book a reality, and for that, I am eternally thankful.

To my wife, Erika, and our daughters,
Valentina and Sofia, you are the center of
my universe!

Author's Note

I was in a boardroom in a downtown Manhattan building. Although I'd done this countless times in the past, this time my mouth was dry, my palms were sweaty, and I was exhausted and extremely nervous. I had been in that room for over 5 hours, explaining how my consulting firm helped businesses sell their offers through worldwide distribution channels.

I painstakingly went over every detail of how my operation worked. I explained exactly how I would recruit industry influencers, introducers, resellers, agents, and brokers as external sales forces and connect them with my clients. My firm's core service was to create a network of sales agents who could open up untapped markets and generate high-volume sales for my clients.

I was revealing all my secrets for optimizing those relationships and accelerating sales. I covered example after example of how my firm would earn money and every way I strategically partnered with my clients. I shared past invoices to demonstrate how I would charge a flat fee for setting up distribution channels and be paid an ongoing percentage of sales revenue. I went over 10 years of strategic partnerships, explaining exactly how they were structured, ranging from Master Agent Agreements, joint venture (JV) partnerships, affiliate frameworks, and every other combination and collaboration I had ever done.

However, this was not a sales presentation because the other people in the boardroom were not prospective clients. I was being interrogated by 2 FBI agents, 2 SEC agents, 2 Assistant District Attorneys, and their supervisor.

In May 2019, the US government indicted me and sentenced me to 4 years in federal prison for aiding and abetting a real estate investment business that defrauded investors of more than $40M. I had recruited a network of 1,200+ worldwide sales agents to sell investments in a commercial real estate business, Bar Works Inc., that built co-working spaces. It was a gut-wrenching blow.

My charge stemmed from my knowledge that the CEO named in the investment brochure was a fabrication. The real CEO had a different identity altogether, yet I knowingly let the fake name circulate among our network of 1200+ sales agents and prospective investors. It's a decision I deeply regret.

I didn't initially know the name was fictitious, but when I found out, I did not disengage the distribution network I had cultivated or specifically alert anyone about the actual individual controlling the business.

The truth is that it was the worst-kept secret, and every staff member at that company knew his real name. A simple Google search on each location's address would show the true registered name against the real estate property. Moreover, the offices were built and occupied, and more locations opened every month. At the time, the business looked good.

I remember feeling weighed down with guilt and a heavy conscience. I knew I wasn't an evil person with bad intentions and had followed the guidance of someone who was more experienced and held a higher rank than me. I trusted their judgment, relying on their expertise to navigate the situation. And then I was betrayed.

But that, I suppose, was bound to happen sooner or later. I had lost my moral compass. And when I lost that compass, I eventually lost everything else. When I say that, people tend to ask, "How much did you lose?" The bottom line is that it's always too much when you lose everything.

Before that, I had learned the power of distribution channels and how to leverage them. It became easier and easier to sell whatever I wanted. I became obsessed with how much money I could make.

I sold everything from recruitment services to real estate offers like land deals, office space, student accommodation, assisted living, boutique hotels, resorts, apartment buildings, and even burial plots. I sold wine, gold, diamonds, and other rare earth metals and precious gems. I bought the rights to sell digital media boards and sold the subsequent advertisement space they provided. Once, I even manufactured and sold my own chocolate bar.

I happily plugged any product or service into this distribution channel strategy I had, watching the money roll in.

Have you ever heard of Icarus, who flew too close to the sun? His wings, which were held together with wax, melted, and he fell to his death... well, that's me, without the dying part, thankfully.

I became so focused on my topline revenue that I cared less and less about what I was selling. It mattered little who I partnered with. All I wanted to know was whether there was a market appetite for the offer and, if so, what my commission would be. I did not slow down to think about whether people could get hurt if I sold a bad product. I wasn't doing any special due diligence on the companies, their owners, or the legalities of who I was partnering with.

Why Me?

I made a lot of money doing this – $800M in sales, and I want to make up for my mistake. Honestly, I could simply focus on my business, doing what I know, and making enough money for my family and me to live comfortably. But I want to pay forward with my skills.

I've had this horrible dream about my daughters being bullied in school. There's a long hallway... the kind that's lined with lockers that students use between classes. My daughters are there, but they can't see me, and I watch as they are picked on and bullied by some other girls. These girls say really mean things like their father is a criminal and a bad person, and they have no right to be in that school – being a criminal is in their blood, and they are criminals, too. It was horrible. This really bad dream crushes my heart and brings me to tears every time I dream it, think about it, or speak it out aloud. I know that I need to change how I'm perceived for the sake of my daughters.

So, I want to share with you how to make your dream of becoming an entrepreneur come true and for you to be successful. I know you want to do this but don't know how.

To be good at something, you need to put in the time and effort, and you also need experience. I became good at what I did because I spent literally thousands of hours direct selling as a salesperson, pitching face-to-face, and learning how to leverage my experience.

Let me share what I've learned and help you succeed and avoid the costly mistake I made. I will give you a recipe for how to positively impact your life and money situation, but you still need to put in the work – point blank, period.

Beware

Look, so many bullshitters are out there talking about how they made money when they are not worth anything. I'm talking about all those, "If you want _____, then here's my system for how I ____. Buy my shitty training program," and they go on and on. They stand in front of *rented* cars and houses, and even worse, they stand in front of fully paid-for houses and cars, for which the money made to pay for those things was from that shitty course they're pushing that won't really help you. They haven't actually done anything.

What I needed was the real deal for how to build a business that makes money long-term and can change your life – not some crappy get-rich-quick scheme like short-term dropshipping or other me-too businesses like eBay or Shopify seller guides or how to be a coach. I'm the person who can help you build something real and that will scale up in direct proportion to the amount of effort you put in! And I'm going to show you how to do that in this book, *The DistroVerse.*

Don't Make My Mistake

But before we jump into the content, it's crucial to highlight the ethical implications of these highly effective strategies. While they can undoubtedly help you generate enormous demand for your products or services, it's important to be aware of the potential challenges that may arise. These strategies are designed to be foolproof, but their immense success can create a unique problem – and by that, I mean meeting the overwhelming demand you create.

Imagine a scenario where your products or services become incredibly popular, and customers are clamoring to make purchases. It sounds like a dream come true, right? However, the reality is that if you're not adequately prepared to meet that demand, you may find yourself in a difficult situation. You could struggle to supply the products or services fast enough to meet the heightened demand.

This predicament can be a double-edged sword. On the one hand, it's a testament to the effectiveness of your strategies. On the other hand, it puts you in a tricky position where you're desperately searching for something to sell quickly. In this rush, there's a risk of compromising your due diligence standards. You may feel pressured to make hasty decisions, neglecting proper research, quality control, or even the legality and ethical aspects of your products or services.

To put it simply, these strategies are like recipes in a cookbook. When you become reasonably proficient at following the instructions, you'll achieve a result that resembles the intended outcome. So just like following a recipe, you don't need to be an expert chef or experienced cook to make the dish look and taste great. Having said that, immediate millionaire status may not be guaranteed either. But you can do really well and earn a lot of money, maybe even hundreds of thousands of dollars or more.

By understanding these potential challenges and maintaining a balanced perspective, you can approach these strategies with caution and integrity. It's vital to prioritize the quality of your offerings, ensure ethical business practices, and uphold your due diligence standards. With the right mindset and approach, you can achieve significant success while maintaining the highest ethical standards.

Let's Get Started

So get set to dive into these powerful strategies, where you'll gain the knowledge to empower yourself, create irresistible offers, and create crazy demand for your business with ease. This book will give you the most simplified, easy-to-understand way to enter any type of business, create a business of your own selling exactly what customers in that market want, at the exact time they want it, and then how to put some rocket fuel in your sales engine to scale your sales up dramatically.

With my proven strategies, you'll unlock the full potential of your business and be on a path to success, leaving your competitors in the dust.

Are you ready?

Is This Book for You?

This book is for people who have been dreaming about leaving their jobs and starting their own businesses but can't shake off the worries about the risks involved. It's also for entrepreneurs, aspiring entrepreneurs, and small business owners who are determined to create a thriving business or take their existing ventures to the next level.

So if you're looking for a solution that directly addresses your concerns and shows you effective ways to mitigate risks, this book is for you.

Here are some key traits of the people I had in mind while writing this book:

- You're ready to step out of your comfort zone and chase your entrepreneurial dreams, even if it means dealing with some uncertainties along the way.
- You highly appreciate guidance and support that is specifically tailored to help you transition from being an employee to becoming a successful entrepreneur.

- You are motivated to invest in resources that can help you overcome the challenges that come with starting your own business, with a plan to finance that.
- You're actively seeking a solution that provides a clear roadmap to success, empowering you to confidently make informed decisions and navigate obstacles.

If you can relate to any of these characteristics, *The DistroVerse* is the perfect book for you. It offers the guidance, support, and strategies you need to pursue your entrepreneurial dreams, manage risks effectively, and build a successful business.

DISCLAIMER: The information in this book comes from my personal experience and knowledge. I am not a licensed legal or financial professional. I generalize this information as guidelines, which are intended to be used for information purposes only and do not constitute professional advice. Please consult independent legal and financial advice for information specific to your country, business, and circumstances. Distro Channels Ltd is not liable to you in any way for your use or reliance on my guidance or the information contained in this book.

Introduction

Hey there! In my book, *The DistroVerse*, I've got your back, whether you're ready to leave your job or simply looking for a come-up in life. This book is designed to empower anyone who wants to step into the world of entrepreneurship and create a path to success. The best part is that I'll show you how to do it with minimal risk and how to start making money right away. Sound good?

This book is split into 4 parts, each building on the previous one to give you the ultimate entrepreneurial success you're after. Whether you're looking for quick income, dreaming of starting your own business, or wanting to scale up your existing venture, *The DistroVerse* has your roadmap to success covered.

Part 1: Empower Yourself, Earn Instantly

Are you ready to take control of your life, work on your own terms, and start generating income immediately? Picture this... what if you could connect with any business and be instantly able to sell their products or services to the exact customers they are trying to sell to? Imagine you didn't even need to do the selling yourself... you could just sort of make it happen, and that they would reward you with generous referral fees or sales commissions for doing so. I'm not talking about getting a job here. No, in this section of the book I'm going to show you 4 steps to becoming your own boss and start making money instantly.

Step 1: I'll show you how to connect with businesses offering lucrative referral programs or sales commissions. This will allow you to quickly sell their offerings and cash in on substantial earnings.

Step 2: You'll learn to negotiate your fee structure to ensure clear expectations and avoid disputes. A well-crafted contract will be your secret weapon, safeguarding your interests.

Step 3: We'll look at the fastest way to strategically target your ideal customers using online platforms and tools designed to pinpoint and engage your target audience. I'll guide you through the process of reaching the right people with precision.

Step 4: Now that you have your offer in place, you've established how you'll be paid, and you know exactly where your target buyers are, I'm going to show you the fastest, most cost-effective way to drive home sales. Here you'll learn to tap into the influence of established networks and influencers to drive your ideal customers directly to the businesses you've partnered with so that you can get paid. *Fast.*

These strategies hold the key to unlocking your potential as a successful entrepreneur, allowing you to start earning from day one. And that's just the beginning.

Part 2: Create Irresistible Offers, On Demand

Now, let's get into the nitty-gritty of starting your own business. You're going to love this part, trust me. We'll find the perfect market that aligns with your passions and skills, I'll show you how to pick and create exactly what to offer, and then I'll show you how to tap into an audience that's already filled with hot prospects who want to buy exactly what you're selling. In Part 2, we're going to turn your dream of building a successful business into a reality.

> **Step 1:** We'll dive into researching different industries to find the one that resonates with you, aligns with your interests, and matches your expertise. No more guesswork – we'll create the market niche that's perfect for you.

> **Step 2:** You have two options to find your audience. You can build your very own audience from scratch, or you can leverage existing audiences in your chosen market. I'm going to show you how to find all the persons, places, and things that already have the attention of the audience you want so you can access them fast.

> **Step 3:** We're going to get up close and personal with your audience to find out what they want. Surveys, polls, direct conversations – you name it. This is all about understanding their needs, desires, and what makes them

tick. It's like having a secret weapon that lets you give them exactly what they need, when they want it.

Step 4: Armed with all that knowledge, we'll create or find products and services that cater to your audience's desires and sell it to them. Think of unique offerings, partnerships with existing solutions, and curating products from different sources. It's time to give your audience exactly what they've been asking for.

Part 3: Accelerate Growth, Drive Up Sales

Now, it's time to take your business to the next level and unlock the key to sustainable growth. In this transformative part of the book, we dive into the strategies that will increase your sales and expand your reach, ensuring your brand becomes an unstoppable force in the market.

Step 1: Position your opportunity as a high-paying venture using the 3X rule. Align your offer with DistroAgents' products or values for strong partnerships.

Step 2: Collaborate effectively and partner with entities that boost your credibility and create a dynamic synergy. We're going to explore collaboration opportunities, sponsorships, and co-marketing initiatives to captivate your audience.

Step 3: Recruit strategically and assemble a team of DistroAgents who drive your DistroNetwork. I'm going to show you how to strategically recruit these agents and tap into their networks for expanded reach and new sales opportunities.

Step 4: Manage and optimize your DistroNetwork by proactively supporting and guiding your DistroAgents for maximum results. Here we're going to motivate top performers and unlock the potential of others to optimize performance for exceptional outcomes.

Part 4: Achieve Massive Scale, Worldwide, 24/7 Nonstop

Reaching DistroUtopia means your DistroNetwork operates like a well-oiled machine, driving your business forward without constant oversight. This part takes everything to a whole new level... it's like an airplane breaking the sound barrier. You were already growing fast, and now we're going to grow even faster!

Step 1: Create a DistroPortal to supercharge your DistroNetwork. This centralized website will serve as a resource hub for all your DistroAgents, providing them with everything they need to perform at their best.

Step 2: Motivate your DistroAgents with a dynamic leaderboard system that promotes healthy competition and fosters a sense of accomplishment. Design your leaderboards to ensure they serve their purpose effectively.

Step 3: Create DistroTeams to amplify results, leveraging the power of teamwork by pairing DistroAgents who complement each other's strengths and have similar target audiences.

Step 4: Adopt a two-tiered model to overcome language barriers and cultural nuances. I'm going to show you how to turn DistroAgents into DistroLeaders who take on the task of finding, recruiting, training, and managing DistroAgents to achieve localized sales efforts and superior customer experiences. This two-tiered approach allows you to focus on strategic decisions and high-level business aspects while your DistroLeaders handle the on-the-ground operations.

Time and time again, I have demonstrated how powerful these strategies are for exponential growth in very short time spans. They work. If you follow them, I promise they will put you ahead of 99% of entrepreneurs, leaving your competitors behind.

Part 1
EMPOWER YOURSELF, EARN INSTANTLY

"Be Your Own Boss and Start Making Money Immediately"

Balancing Dreams and Reality

I remember when I first started aspiring to become a super successful businessperson, visualizing the kind of life success would provide. I thought about the material things at first – the money, the cars, and the lifestyle. I could almost feel how having a successful business would make me more attractive and influential. I could even imagine the pride of having a legacy I could hand down to the next generation.

Those powerful emotions had me consuming anything and everything I could get my hands on about success, building businesses, leadership, and money making. I'd buy books, order training programs, read magazines, and watch shows like *The Apprentice* and *Dragons' Den*, the UK equivalent of *Shark Tank*. I watched *Shark Tank*, too. On top of all that self-help, money-making, and startup media I was consuming, I also went to school and university for business studies.

What made these books, seminars, lectures, and shows so addictive had a lot to do with how romantically those business personalities, teachers, gurus, and entrepreneurs spoke about startups. They would say things that made them sound so cool and sexy like, "Oh, with startups, you just have to go for it, it's make or break" and "When I built my business, it was like jumping out of an airplane without a parachute and having to make one on the way down before you go splat." Others suggested, "Sometimes, it's better *not* to have a safety net so that, you know, failure is not an option, just climb and stay focused on the goal, sometimes that's just what it takes."

Any concern with startup costs was met with some variation of the response, "You've got to speculate to accumulate." And the one that bugs me the most, "What's the worst that can happen, if you fail, you can always simply get a job." Well, the harsh reality is that you can be a lot worse off than simply choosing to get a job again. Many bad things can befall an entrepreneur whose business doesn't go as planned.

I've personally learned through countless experiences to tread carefully because you could find yourself so broke and in so much debt that you'll never be able to pay it off. You could have legal issues if you've fallen afoul of regulations, permits, or licensing, subjecting you to fines and other penalties, large payouts, and/or expensive civil dispute litigation. You might inadvertently find yourself on the wrong side of the law and face criminal charges. It happens more often than you might know. Misstepping in the pursuit of money is easy to do, and the repercussions of bad decisions and plans gone wrong are endless.

But of course, these aren't the things you focus on in the beginning.

Going It Alone

I was coming up with lots of business ideas, which I thought were innovative and well-thought-out. But the trouble was that despite coming up with all those ideas, I was never truly passionate about any of them – there was no one "Big Problem" I was trying to fix. And when I reached a point where I had chosen a "Big Problem" to tackle, my "Solution" was never really that good. On closer inspection or when taking the first few steps with the startup, I usually found that most of my "Solutions" were unrealistic, super-complex, already done, technologically impossible, or something I was plainly not knowledgeable in, qualified in, experienced in, or even licensed to explore. It turns out there are many regulatory roadblocks to contend with in fields like medical, legal, and financial.

Take this example. You know how people want second opinions or something double-checked before making a decision? Well I had this cool idea for an app called The Lookover, which used a peer review model where people and businesses could post something that would be looked over by others to make better, more informed decisions. Well, that was easier said than done! And while it's still a pretty good idea, now there are these AI models that are becoming smarter by the second. They can sift through information, make complex stuff simple to understand, and provide suggestions. You can feed them documents and ask them to point out where things might not match up or where you might be on the losing side.

So, while the idea behind The Lookover is still cool, bringing it to life would require Silicon Valley-level venture capital funding and top-tier tech partnerships. Plus, AI tools like ChatGPT can do it already, and it's accessible to almost everyone, at a low to no cost.

For me, these ideas were simply fantasies. It was like I kept myself following the proverbial carrot with myself, knowingly holding up the stick. I kept fantasizing about those businesses and the accompanying lifestyle they'd bring because the fantasy itself got me through the reality of dealing with low prospects, the insufferable job I had, and the crappy place I lived in.

What I really needed was a way to find my footing and take that first step to create my own business. To do that, I needed a step-by-step plan, like a cooking recipe which would show me how to start a business that would pay me enough to live. That became my goal. I wanted to work to live, not live to work.

I knew that if I could take my first small step successfully, become independent, and sustain it, I would be able to take more and more steps toward building the business I imagined, whatever business that may be.

I no longer wanted to hear about those successful entrepreneurs who embarked on those long, ever-evolving journeys to the top. I became tired of the same old stories about how they re-invented themselves, overcoming huge debt, poverty, relationship issues, and hostile competitors, all the while showing off their happy families, impeccable lifestyles, and mastery of the ever-coveted work-life balance.

It actually became annoying to listen to people emphasize their many years of experience or attribute their success to a highly unusual habit they formed, as if waking up stupidly early in the morning to get a head start on your day was some kind of superpower. Many gurus get your attention by representing something completely unconnected to business but argue that the subject has something to teach entrepreneurs.

I'm being intentionally vague here, but you might find some of these familiar. Some preach that unimaginable success was within reach if I only followed a new habit like keeping my work week under 4 hours, keeping daily planners, writing promises to myself about financial goals, looking at images of the life I want, or meditating or other cognitive exercises that supposedly train my mind to tap into the ethereal, unknown, intangible law of attraction.

Admittedly, some of those practices are genuinely helpful for motivation, preparedness, discipline, and overall focus. Perhaps that's the point, and by doing all those things, you become more likely to be able to pounce on an opportunity when it arises as opposed to missing the opportunity altogether.

But for me, the trouble was the lack of a definitive set of instructions like you have when assembling a set of drawers from IKEA, a cookbook recipe to follow, or a script to go by. I needed a step-by-step guide, where if I followed those exact steps to the best of my ability, I could expect to achieve a certain result within reasonable parameters.

Oh, and by the way, I admit (especially after that rant!) that it is a little cliché or borderline hypocritical that I am aligning myself with those gurus by writing this book. The reality is that learning from others who have done it before you will always be important for preparation and guidance. However, my point is that there comes a time when you need to stop consuming knowledge to feed your fantasy and actually take positive action. I hope this book will spur you into action – perhaps Part 1: Empower Yourself, Earn Instantly, in and of itself, will do it. In fact, if you don't feel an overwhelming sense of urgency to take some positive action toward your business dream by the end of it, I'd say it's safe for you to put this book down and do better things with your time.

Discover the Recipe

I remember when I was at a gas station with my dad when I was young and asked him to buy me some gum. And for the first time, he told me to buy it by myself. I'd seen him buy stuff all the time, so I pretty much knew the process. But since this was my first time, I was extremely nervous and felt like I didn't know what to do or say. But then my dad started to guide me, telling me what to say and what to do. He literally gave me a script to follow. Step one was to pick up the gum I wanted. Step two was to place the gum on the counter and greet the shopkeeper, explaining how I would like to buy that gum. He told me to say verbatim, "Hello miss, I would like to buy this gum, please." Step three was to wait for the shopkeeper to tell me how much it was. Step four was for me to see if I had enough money, and so on.

Scripts like that are so helpful. For me, it took the fear and doubt out of the equation. I knew what to say and when to say it. I had a set of instructions, which if I followed, would give me an expected result. I needed this type of instruction for starting a business and taking control of my own income. That would show me how unimaginable success was within my reach, and if I followed a certain path, to the best of my ability, I would start seeing that fantasy becoming reality.

So in real terms, I wanted a business in a box, the instant noodles for startups, the one-click startup with the Amazon-style next-day delivery option.

And I found a way to do it, which I will share with you now. I found it to be low cost or no cost so that you can comfortably slide into self-employment and put yourself firmly in charge of your own income in a way that actually gets you paid! This is the first step in your business journey, and you'll see how the trajectory can lead you to something bigger if you stay the course.

It was September 2008, and I was walking out of yet another interview, knowing full well I wouldn't get the job. After graduating from university with a second upper (2:1) in Business Enterprise and Management, I spent the entire summer applying for jobs and going to interviews in London. A second upper, by the way, is a fancy way of saying I received a B+. And the university I went to wasn't anything to rave about either. Suffice it to say that my average qualifications from an average university didn't have me sitting confidently in an interview waiting room filled with other hopeful candidates who were all top of their class from top-tier universities like Oxford and Cambridge.

Graduate job interviews are known to be tough with fierce competition, but things were especially hard in 2008 since it was also a time when the whole world was smack bang in the middle of a global recession. Most companies at that time were not hiring at all, especially for inexperienced graduates. For the few firms that were hiring, they were overwhelmed and inundated with applications and could, therefore, pick and choose from the very best.

I walked out of that interview feeling defeated and desperate. I was broke and couldn't even afford the travel costs for getting into the city for interviews. I was applying for jobs blindly by this point and could barely keep track of which companies I had applied to or which recruitment agency I was supposed to follow up with. I had to think of something. I needed to put aside my idea of being hired by a fancy global corporate finance or consulting firm and figure out how to put money in my pocket now!

It was about 20 minutes after I walked out of that interview when it hit me. The recruitment consultant from the agency who landed me the interview called to see if I had been offered the job. Apart from giving him the bad news, I suddenly had a moment of clarity and re-evaluated my situation. I had essentially walked into that interview with a price tag around my neck. All the recruiter had done was find a company that had a vacancy and was willing to pay someone else to find them a suitable candidate. The recruiter I was talking to (and the others before him) had a simple agreement in place to be paid a commission if they found someone for the job.

At that moment, I realized I could do that, too. I simply needed to find a company that would agree to pay me a fee for getting them something they wanted – and it didn't need to be recruitment services either.

The train ride back from central London to Croydon, south London, where I lived, was different this time. I wasn't deflated! Instead, I was thinking of ways I could strategically position myself between businesses and the things they wanted. I started to think about all the small local business owners who I thought would pay referral fees or some other commission for an introduction that becomes profitable for them.

I recalled all the companies I'd recently been in contact with that had asked me for a referral in some way. I thought about the dentist who had asked me for a referral for their teeth-whitening service. I remembered the local solicitors (lawyers) asking for referrals, too. The same goes for my local accountant, the web design company and small advertising agencies, the PR and event planners, and even the training companies, small gyms, and personal trainers.

My mind was buzzing with ideas! Would an expensive hair salon pay me a flat fee for bringing them a customer? And would a health club pay me a percentage of a membership enrollment fee if I brought them a new member? Better still, would they pay me an ongoing monthly commission for the lifetime of that member? Would a restaurant pay me an event planner fee if I brought them large groups to dine, and would swanky nightclubs pay me a promoter fee for bringing them a VIP guest or people who would pay for VIP treatment?

The answer is YES to everything, and the list of options kept growing because most businesses wanted referrals. It was a no-lose situation for all those businesses because they would only pay me if I bought them a paying customer.

For me to do this, I followed 4 steps:

1. Call a business.
2. Agree on a fee or commission for sending them a buyer.
3. Locate their ideal customers.
4. Start signposting those customers.

Step 1: Contact a Business

If you were to follow the same process, the first step is to choose a business you want to partner with. I would start by looking for companies that would be happy to pay you a referral fee or sales commission as a reward for bringing them a paying customer.

Here's the thing, you're going to find many businesses that will be agreeable with this deal. Think about it, when you bring a business a paying customer and they do not have to pay any money in staff expenses or advertising to acquire them, they are usually more than happy to reward you for the referral.

Imagine walking into a local car dealership and telling the owner:

> *I know a few people who want to buy cars right now. I've spoken to them, and I've gotten them interested in some of the models you carry here at your dealership. Would you mind if I brought them in to buy some of your cars?*

Do you think they'd object to that offer? In fact, what dealership do you know that would say no to that offer? It's free money for them. They've made a sale without having to lift a finger. You found the customers, you took care of the sales part, and then you brought them to the dealership on a silver platter.

They probably wouldn't want you to stop at all!

If they're not trying to hire you on the spot, they are probably thinking of what reward they can offer you to incentivize you to continue bringing them customers like that. Even if you asked them to pay you the same sales commission they pay their own staff, they'd probably be okay with it because they're still up!

They didn't have to pay you any wages, provide you with health insurance, or train you. They simply paid you a commission on a completed sale! It's a no-lose situation for them.

Because of that dynamic, you need to be selective about who you partner with. Since most businesses will accept the customers you refer, it's important to factor in a few things to ensure the reward is big enough and easy enough to be worth your time and energy. This is especially true if it will cost you money to get the customers.

My advice is that whatever company you choose to partner with, it's best to choose one where you can:

1. Sell a lot of what they offer really fast or
2. Sell something where you only need one or two sales per month.

So if you're looking for something you can sell really fast, then you need to make sure there's enough supply for you to work with. Also, if it's something that's relatively low cost, then you can potentially get more customers quicker, too, since they are more affordable and have a broader appeal. On top of that, the higher volume in sales also helps you build your own brand faster and penetrate the market.

Or, you could choose businesses that sell expensive items or services where they can pay you more money for your help. Selling things that cost a lot usually means you can earn bigger commissions, which makes your work more worthwhile. You could try to find businesses that sell pricey stuff, like luxury products, high-end tech stuff, or specialized professional services. These kinds of businesses often have more money to give you for bringing them customers because they make more profit on what they sell.

For example, introducing someone to a specialty cake shop you've partnered with to buy a wedding cake may not be the best idea because, despite how expensive the cake is, you'd only be selling one. How much can you earn from selling one cake? Unless that cake were thousands of dollars, you wouldn't make very much. Even if you had a few people who wanted wedding cakes, you're also limited by the number of cakes they can bake on demand. However, if you partnered with a wedding planner who usually bills thousands of dollars to plan a wedding event, your reward as a commission could be much, much more.

I'm not suggesting you only work with local car dealerships and wedding planners, either. What I am suggesting is that you stick to smaller privately owned businesses that will likely place much more value on your contribution.

In fact, you can go beyond the street-facing brick-and-mortar businesses in your area and work with online businesses that sell nationally where location is not a factor. In the beginning, I recommend focusing on local businesses. But if you want to work with an online business, try selecting a smaller one. That's what I did. When I did it this way, I had a higher likelihood of getting an exclusive arrangement with them, plus it reduces the competition for people selling to the same audience. It's way better to be the sole external promoter or at least one of a small group.

And if you set this up correctly and deliver amazing results, you have the potential for the company you chose to create your own unique offer with them. You could enhance the product, add additional features, or even package it differently to create a more appealing option for your customers. This allows you to increase the product's value, which means you can also increase its price point. A higher price benefits you and your partner company. You'll both stand to make more money on sales, and you'll even be in the position to negotiate a higher commission.

This is a different type of arrangement, which I fully unpack in Part 2: Creating Irresistible Offers, On Demand. But to summarize it quickly here, when you are in a position to negotiate this type of arrangement, you can also secure exclusive distribution rights, making you the sole seller of this improved product.

Exclusivity like this is powerful in setting yourself apart from everybody else as it not only differentiates you from competitors but also adds a sense of uniqueness and rarity to your product, which can further drive up demand.

However, don't expect a partner company to create a new offer like this and give you exclusive distribution rights without sending them a ton of business. It's not something that will be handed to you on a silver platter. You need to demonstrate your capability and commitment. Show the company that you have the market knowledge, the customer base, and the marketing skills to make this product a success. If you're consistently delivering results and proving your value as a partner, companies are generally more open to working with you on exclusive deals.

The good news is that I'm about to show you how to get to that stage. So, pay attention!

Create the List

I wish I could tell you exactly which companies to approach, but since I'm not with you right now, I cannot make that recommendation. But if I were with you, I'd first ask you to make a list of all the businesses you think would be a good fit for you. For this, we would rely on your memory and familiarity with businesses around you and the private brands you've already come across.

Next, we would find a list of local businesses to start scanning through. A quick Google search for "[Town/City] business directory" should give you some options to get started. You could even be more specific to the industry, product, or service you like and search for something like "high-end jewelry stores [Town/City]." By the way, you don't need to limit yourself to local companies. I suggested local places because they will be familiar to you, so you'll start thinking of options quickly. But honestly, you can also search for any online-only business or even businesses around the world. This strategy is actually that awesome.

The third thing I'd have you do is try a hack I've used successfully. Go to a job listing site, such as Indeed, Monster, ZipRecruiter, and even Craigslist, and search for businesses with sales-oriented job listings in your desired location. The great thing about these job boards is that you can search job listings by area and specialty, meaning you can see which businesses of all sizes have been actively hiring in the exact geographical location you want, in the industry sector you want, and if they are looking for salespeople. If they need salespeople, they're willing to pay someone to find them the ideal customers they're looking for.

There are a few extra things you can glean from these job-site listings. The job description usually summarizes what the business does, what they sell, and what caliber salesperson they're looking for. How much money they are willing to pay in salary and bonuses is a good indicator of your earning potential. On the face of it, you know they are willing to pay to get customers to buy their stuff. It tells you that they are financially stable enough to hire salespeople and are an active business. It will also indicate the company's size.

As you're researching and building your list, remember that you're looking at these job listings through a different lens. You are not looking for a job with a basic salary. You're looking for a partnership, not an interview. You are not a hopeful candidate contacting HR anymore. The tables have turned – you are the empowered one because you are someone who's going to refer them paying customers. And because of that, you get to speak to the owners.

Pro Tip

Don't look at recruitment agency listings. Instead, look for jobs listed by employers only. There's usually a button on most job search sites allowing you to toggle whether you want to include recruiter listings. Select the "do not include" option.

These three suggested lists won't show you all your options, but it's a good place to start. Branch off as your mind learns what's out there. Collate these in one master list of businesses you want to partner with.

Make Contact

Once you have that master list, don't waste any time. Start the ball rolling immediately!

Pick up the phone, call the number on the company website, and say the following:

> *Hi, my name is [Your Name], and I have a [Client/Customer] I would like to send to you, and I would like to be paid a referral fee when they buy your [Product/Service]. Who can I discuss this with, or do you already have an introducer, referral, or affiliate program set up for this?*

It was that simple, and for 9 out of 10 calls like this, the receptionist would transfer me to someone I could negotiate with and discuss ways I could collaborate.

When I was put through, I'd say something like:

> *Hi, my name is [Your Name], and I've been following your business since [Date], and I think your [Product/Service] would fit the [People/Audience] I work with. In fact, I shared [Quick Reference about Product/Service] to my [People/Audience]*

and received a great response! I'd like to refer business to you. Would you be open to discussing some options I have in mind?

If I were asked to email the person I needed to talk to, which tends to happen more often than not, I wrote a similar email:

Hi [Prospect's Name],

My name is [Your Name], and I've been following your company since [Date].

Your [Product/Service], in particular, resonates with my [People/Audience]. In fact, I shared [Quick Reference about Product/Service] with my [People/Audience] and received a fantastic response.

I wanted to get in touch about referring business to you and working together in a non-competitive but profitable way for both of us.

If you're open to a conversation about that, I'd like to set up a phone call this week to discuss some collaboration ideas I have in mind.

When would you be available for a quick call? I'm available at [Contact Info].

Would [Date/Time] work for you?

Kind regards,
[Your Name]

Is This Affiliate Marketing?

You might be thinking hey, this sounds like affiliate marketing, and you wouldn't be wrong. This strategy can incorporate affiliate marketing but also other types of marketing collaborations, such as joint ventures, introducer agreements, referral partner programs, reselling agent agreements, distributorship, influencer partnerships, licensing agreements, business development partnerships, and even co-branding initiatives. More on this later in the book.

So before moving on, while we're on the subject of affiliate marketing, let's quickly cover affiliate marketplaces!

You have the option to use affiliate websites that specialize in high-ticket niches. The advantage here is that these businesses are already familiar with the value of referral marketing and are prepared to offer more generous compensation for leads or sales. This approach can be more time efficient and connects you directly with businesses that understand and value high-quality referrals.

However, identifying high-ticket affiliate programs can be a bit difficult because not all sites will actually categorize their offerings as "high-ticket." However, there are a few affiliate marketplaces that are known for hosting programs which include or specialize in products or services with higher price points, which in turn offers the potential for bigger commission payouts.

Here are a few I know about:

- **Avangate Affiliate Network** specializes in software and SaaS products, which often come with higher price tags and commissions.
- **CJ Affiliate** includes several luxury brands and high-end products, particularly in technology, home appliances, and travel packages.
- **ClickBank** is known for a wide range of products and also features high-ticket items, especially in niches like business and marketing courses, personal development, and health and fitness programs.
- **Impact** is known for its variety of high-end brands and products, especially in the technology and luxury goods sectors.
- **JVZoo** focuses mainly on digital products with high-ticket offerings, particularly in business and marketing tools, software, and online courses.
- **ShareASale** has high-ticket items in categories like home and garden (luxury furniture, high-end home appliances), business services, and premium fashion brands.

Now you know where to find affiliate programs, so don't say I didn't tell you about them. But here's my problem with affiliate sites... they are also well known among ALL other professional (and unprofessional) affiliates, which means you could be up against a lot of competition. This can, and will, seriously dilute the value of each affiliate's effort, which makes it much harder to secure those lucrative deals.

Let's now compare that to my reasons for choosing to work with smaller private businesses that are not accustomed to referral partner programs or affiliate programs. They have:

- **Less competition**: Smaller businesses, especially those not extensively using affiliate networks, will probably have a lot less competition with other external people selling their stuff. This allows for a more personalized and direct relationship with the business, which increases the chances of securing a deal.

- **Greater appreciation for individual efforts**: Smaller businesses will probably value your contribution a lot more if they're not used to a large amount of leads and sales from multiple affiliates. Your efforts in bringing them business may be seen as more significant, which could lead to potentially better rewards.

- **Flexibility in negotiating terms**: With smaller private businesses, you might have more room to negotiate the partnership terms. This flexibility can lead to more favorable conditions than standardized affiliate programs.

- **Building long-term relationships**: Working directly with smaller businesses allows for the development of long-term relationships. This can lead to exclusive deals, which you won't get in a crowded affiliate marketplace.

Finally, if you want to avoid the manual effort of searching for businesses yourself, check out the DistroList Marketplace listings. It's a place where our DistroAgents have already picked and pre-vetted business opportunities. By looking at what's available in the DistroList Marketplace, you can save time and go straight to good options, instead of searching everywhere by yourself. When you do this, you're also integrating yourself into the DistroVerse ecosystem, which moves you away from the process of manual searching.

I explain this in more depth as we advance through the book, but you could also list the businesses you've found within the marketplace, too. The listing invites other DistroList members to view these opportunities. This could encourage them to build out distribution networks or integrate your opportunities into their existing networks. It's a powerful way to expand your reach and make the most of the resources at your disposal. That was a shameless plug. I know. Sorry not sorry.

Action Plan

Create the List

- Brainstorm on local businesses you already know.
- Search online directories, social media, and local networking events, focusing on privately owned businesses.
- Search recruiting sites hiring salespeople in your location.

Make Contact

- Call or email the businesses to ask about a partnership or referral program.
- Mention potential customers who are interested in their products or services.
- Propose a phone call to discuss collaboration options.

Assess Compatibility and Value

- Evaluate each business for compatibility with your target audience.
- Research the business' financial stability.
- Ensure the earnings will be worth your efforts.

Create Engaging Messages

- Highlight the mutual benefits of collaboration.
- Customize your message to each business.
- Mention interested potential customers.

Final Step

- Follow up with businesses showing interest.

Step 2: Agree to a Fee

When I contacted local businesses in this way, I was always able to have a meaningful conversation about how we could collaborate.

Business owners can often become overly creative (in a bad way) if you leave it up to them to structure the collaboration. So, to keep ideas on planet Earth, I used the same options recruitment agencies give companies when they recruit viable candidates for a job opening.

Recruitment consultants usually give companies one of two options, depending on whether the role is temporary or permanent. For a permanent position, a recruitment consultant will charge the equivalent of 10-15% of a successful candidate's first-year salary. For temporary positions, the payment will be an ongoing percentage of an hourly wage.

For me, that would be negotiating for either:

1. A one-time fee for referring the client (a flat fee or percentage of the total value of what was sold) or
2. A recurring payment on a continuity product or service (usually 20-30% of a monthly payment).

I tied this arrangement down with a contract, providing me with some peace of mind that all the transactions followed a predefined agreement I could rely on. This part of the process is really important because it is made crystal clear what needs to be delivered for fees and compensation to be paid and that any issues and disputes can be resolved. After all, what was agreed upon is in black and white in a signed contract.

I'm not surprised if you think writing a contract will be overwhelming. There can be a lot of things a contract needs to cover, especially if agreements are complex. I always recommend seeking legal advice when creating a contract to ensure everything is covered.

However, in the fledgling stage of your business, which at this stage is really more like a solo pursuit in giving yourself a raise in the form of money earned outside of your normal 9-5, it's not always necessary to have lawyers creating a monster-size contract. When I first started out, I didn't have the money for a lawyer, so I put together my own agreement that was legally binding and professional.

A typical introducer agreement, referral agreement, affiliate, or influencer contract can be broken down into 7 sections that will be legally binding when agreed upon and signed. Over the last decade, with hundreds of thousands of dollars spent on lawyers to create contracts, I realized that these 7 sections are the backbone of all my referral introducer and joint venture agreements. Obviously, these 7 sections don't cover every angle, so if you feel you need more disclosures or protective writing, contact a lawyer to tailor make you a contract.

To give you something to get you going immediately (and I really did this when I started), follow the next 7 steps, and you'll have a great starting contract. You can literally do this on the back of an envelope or napkin.

1. **Names, Signatories, and Date:** List the names and signatories of both parties entering into the contract and the date when the contract is agreed upon.

    This referral agreement is entered into [Effective Date] by and between [Name] with the address of [Address] (the Company) and [Name] with the address of [Address] (the Referrer), collectively the parties.

2. **Short Description:** This is an introductory paragraph describing what the contact is for.

    Upon the effective date of this referral agreement, the referrer may, from time to time, refer potential clients/customers to the company. The company will pay a fee for these referrals.

3. **Timelines, Deadlines, and Contract Length:** State the length of the contract, including the start date and end date. If it's going to be an ongoing relationship, this is the area to state that.

    This agreement shall commence upon the effective date as stated above until [Date].

4. **Deliverables:** Define the specific value exchange to be performed.

    The company shall pay the referrer for each successful referral, where a successful referral is defined as a referral that becomes a client/customer of the company.

5. **Fees and Compensation:** Specify the agreed-upon fees and compensation, and clearly state how payments will be made and when they are due.

    The company shall pay the referrer (a Fee of [Fee] or [Percent] of the total value of a completed sale) within 30 days of a completed referral, where the completed referral will be the engagement of a new client/customer.

6. **Confidentiality Agreement:** Specify what you do not want to be disclosed to any third parties.

    Any financial agreements, strategies, marketing plans, and any other material or information related to this agreement must not be disclosed to third parties.

7. **Declaration and Signatures:** All signatory parties must sign the contract acknowledging that they have read the document and agree to the terms.

    By signing this agreement, all parties agree to the terms disclosed above, [Name], [Date] and [Name], [Date].

Pro Tip

In our rapidly evolving world, the way we make contracts is also changing. In the past, it needed extensive legal consultation and manual drafting, or for simpler stuff, you could use services like Rocket Lawyer, LegalZoom, and LawDepot. But now, technology has changed everything, especially with AI tools. You could use ChatGPT to build yourself a contract right now with a prompt that encompasses everything I've just explained about contracts with something like this:

Can you help me draft a contract for an introducer agreement between [Your Business Name] and [Other Party's Name], detailing [Brief Description of Agreement], for [Duration of Contract], and specifying [What You Expect from Each Party], including the [FEES] involved? Please include sections about confidentiality and signatures. I want it to be clear and simple to understand.

This contract ensures you will be paid. Once both parties sign the contract, it makes the contract binding, and they accept the repercussions of breaking any terms in the contract.

Whether you are collecting a flat fee for referring a customer or an ongoing percentage of a monthly subscription a referral purchased, you only need to send an invoice stating how much is due. And you can expect to be paid as per the terms agreed upon in your contract.

When collecting a percentage of a bill that might differ each month, you could request a copy of that customer/client bill at the end of each month so that you know how much to invoice. For example, if you had an agreement with an accountant that you would receive 10% of the billings of any client you referred, you would use this approach.

This should give you a good basis for ensuring your business relationships are smooth. Also, having contracts in place embeds a sense of professionalism, which requires that the business you collaborate with operates in the same fashion.

What I've explained so far is what you would need to do when approaching local brick-and-mortar businesses. Many companies already have a process or system set up to accommodate this type of collaboration. Businesses see the no-risk, win-win advantages of this setup, too. They may have streamlined this process so that they have dedicated staff, entire departments, and even purpose-built customer acquisition tracking systems with automated payouts set up for you. In fact, you'll find this commonplace where a company has an established affiliate, referral, or introducer program in place.

Remember when we talked about affiliate marketplaces? Look at those examples or even Amazon Affiliates to see what I mean. You could even Google "top affiliate programs for influencers" for a mountain of other options, too. You'll find some with simple and easy agreements to very complex, restrictive, exclusivity-driven options with tiered payouts and even setup fees, which start to look more like network marketing or multilevel marketing businesses. But that's the mainstream. Again, you'd be competing with far too many people. It's like that old saying, "Stick to the path less traveled as it's usually paved with gold." I have suggested that you stick with small-to-medium private businesses that are local to you. This is the first baby step in your journey to the top, so stick to the small businesses for now. That's the way I started.

Action Plan

Propose Collaboration Structures

- Clearly articulate the value you can offer and highlight how collaboration can benefit both parties.
- Present simple options, such as a one-time referral fee or a fixed percentage of sales.
- Explain the advantages of each structure and how it aligns with their business goals.

Prepare a Basic Contract

- Create a basic contract using a template or online resources.
- Include the 7 essential sections – names, signatories, dates; what the contract is for; timeline; deliverables; fees and compensation; confidentiality; and declaration and signatures.
- Ensure clarity and mutual understanding but keep the contract relatively simple.

Review and Negotiate

- Discuss the contract terms with the collaborating business.
- Address any concerns or questions.
- Negotiate terms to ensure both parties are satisfied and the contract is fair.

Contract Signing

- Once all parties are comfortable with the contract terms, sign and date the agreement.

- Ensure all signatories have read and understood the document.
- Store the agreement in a place where you can easily access it.

Advanced Difficulty

- Some deals are more complex. The difficulty level of the action plan depends on your experience, resources, and the complexity of the collaborations you seek. You may require expert guidance.

Seek Legal Advice

- Engage a lawyer to review your contract.
- Develop custom contracts that account for specific collaboration scenarios.
- Include additional sections and clauses based on the agreement complexity.

Explore Advanced Collaboration Structures

- Investigate more intricate fee structures, such as tiered payouts or performance-based incentives.
- Engage in partnerships that require exclusivity or have extensive obligations.
- Implement a two-tiered licensing model to bring on promoters and expand your reach.

Step 3: Find Ideal Customers

Don't have a personal network of ideal customers to tap into? No problem!

By this point, you might be doing what I did and are already searching for local businesses that you could come to an arrangement with. You might already be making a list and guessing how much you think they would be willing to pay you if you referred someone.

But what if the size of your social circle and personal network of contacts is not big enough, and you don't know anyone you could refer to those businesses? Or you quickly realize (as I did) that I would run out of people to refer pretty quickly because, frankly, the size of my social circles and network of contacts was not actually that big.

Sure, I might have been able to come to a nice agreement with a local luxury jewelry store where they'd agreed to pay me 25% on any watch sold above $5,000. And maybe I'd get one or two people who earned enough money to afford something like that *and* were in the market, at that exact time, for a luxury watch. But after that, I'd have no one else to refer.

If that is the case for you, don't be disheartened because there's a solution for that. All you need to do is figure out who that business' ideal customer is. Once you've done that, it's quite easy to find them and start signposting.

Who Is Your Ideal Customer?

It's like when a company wants to hire for a position. They put out a job advert and a job description. Within that job description, a candidate profile spells out exactly what that company wants from their ideal candidate. It might say things like they want a successful candidate to be comfortable with travel, college-educated, and proficient with PowerPoint and Keynote presentations. They may want people with no less than 7 years of experience within a specific field with a mathematics-based educational background. They can, and do, get very specific. But as a recruiter, once you know the ideal candidate profile, it's a relatively straightforward process to go about finding suitable candidates.

It's the same deal with finding your ideal customer, too. Since you don't have a job description per se, you will have to work off other factors that signal whether someone might be interested in what you are selling. At my workshops and events, I often ask people who their ideal customer is. I usually get answers like "people who love fitness," "anyone with a car," and "anyone who earns over 6 figures." This is all much too vague!

Let me put it to you differently… you know how when you know someone really well, like a close relative or a friend, you know exactly what to get them for their birthday? Well, you know what gift to give them because you know things like what their favorite hobbies are, whether they like to read or not, what music they like, how old they are, and their income level. You'll even know details like what they might consider an expensive gift, what they may think is cheap, or even what they think is a thoughtful and meaningful gift.

That is how you need to know your customer. The more you know about them, the less time and money you waste finding and selling to them. The good news is that the internet and social media platforms have made that kind of intimate knowledge about people available to businesses.

That means you can easily make your equivalent of a candidate profile because you can get really specific results based on demographics, social information, and behavioral data.

For example, your ideal customer could be a woman, aged between 25 and 45, single, rents in Manhattan, New York, college-educated, and earns over six figures. These are your demographics. Then for your social and behavioral information, you might want to know if they like running and have ever been interested in or have taken part in the New York Marathon. You may want to know if they have interests in indoor cycling, yoga, and other types of self-care. Maybe you want to know whether they are using dating apps and if they recently liked romantic comedies. These attributes and interests can be easily searched and marketed to.

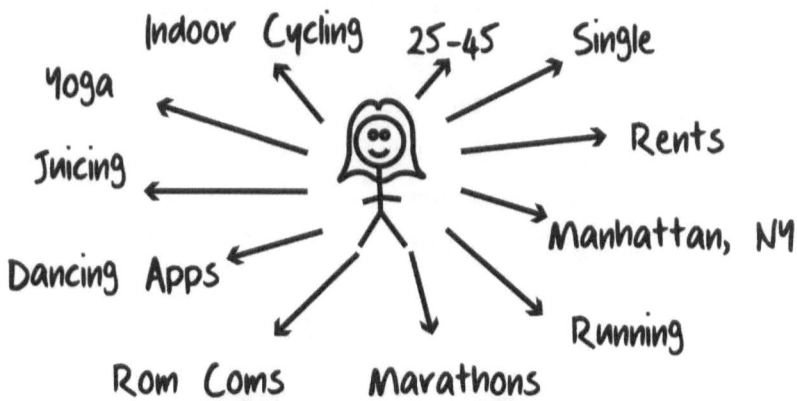

When you put this information together, can you see how it can start to give you a clear picture of your ideal customer? When you know your customer like this, you know exactly what to say, what to offer, and where to advertise, which means you know where to put up your signposts! You'll be able to find them, get their attention, and convert them into buyers. Your job right now is to write down your ideal customer's demographics and social and behavioral traits.

To put you on the right path, start by answering the following questions:

- How old are they?
- Where do they live?
- What is their gender profile?
- What is their race or ethnicity?
- How much do they earn?
- Are they a homeowner or renter?
- What is their education level?
- What kind of job do they have?
- Do they have kids? If so, how many and how old?
- Are they married, divorced, separated, or single?
- Do they prefer audio, video, or written content?
- Which sites do they go to?
- Which apps do they use?
- Which podcasts do they listen to?
- Which shows do they watch?
- What do they do for fun?
- What are their hobbies?

The more questions and answers you can come up with will give you a much better picture of who your ideal customer is and make it easier to find them. The answers to these questions will act as the keywords, interests, search phrases, and clues for finding out where your ideal customers are.

With this information, you can literally go into certain platforms, type in those keywords and interests, and find your ideal customers.

For example, Google and Facebook have ad managers that provide all those audience search functions and more. You can create an ad from either of those platforms and have it reach millions of your ideal customers. This can be a very expensive way to do it. I don't recommend starting that way, but it illustrates my point.

DistroList.app, a platform I built, helps you discover where your ideal customers gather both online and offline. No longer limited to searching social media platforms, DistroList.app generates a comprehensive list of potential places frequented by your target audience. With this valuable insight, you can now explore and find the persons, places, and things that exist within these locations. That means you can find the influencers your customers trust, the events they attend, and the products they buy. These partners could signpost your ideal customers directly to you.

When I first started out, I decided that the easiest thing to do was choose a business based on the wants and needs of the people in my social circles and close network of contacts. At that time, my network was full of recent graduates, young professionals, and budding entrepreneurs. Some of them were close friends, but most of them were mutual acquaintances, friends-of-friends, colleagues, and generally people with similar interests, both professionally and socially. They spent time on the same Facebook groups and forum discussions. They tended to follow the same social media personalities and influencers and liked the same kinds of posts and visited the same type of sites. And because of all that social relatedness, they (we) were all susceptible to similar advertisements that promoted social norms, new trends, and even temporary fads.

Since many of us were at a similar point in our life cycles, we also shared similar social and professional pressures. Many of us wanted to find a job with a career path that matched our aspirations, some of us were working on building a startup (because having a startup is cool and meant to eventually make you rich), and we wanted to stay fit, socialize, party, and travel the world.

So, recognizing that, I started contacting local career consultants, real estate agents, advertising agencies, health clubs, gyms, night clubs, event companies, and even travel agencies that offered specially packaged vacations for the 18-30 age range. I was trying to find any company that would cater to the wants and needs of that buyer group, my ideal customers.

Before I go into the next section on how and where to put up those signposts to start directing your ideal customers, I have a question for you. Have you answered the questions I posed earlier in this section yet?

If the answer is no, then I don't think I've properly expressed how important this step is. Stop what you're doing for a minute, and look at how far you've come. You found a company you want to work with. You contacted them and pitched whoever is in charge how you want to be paid for sending them a paying customer, which they agreed to! Then you negotiated your fee and contracted the agreement... that's pretty impressive. That's something to celebrate in and of itself! Give yourself some credit.

But now the question is *WHO* will buy what you're promoting? Who? Who? Who?

If you read that out loud, you'd sound like an owl. If you're listening to this as an audiobook, then I sound like the owl... I hope this gets my point across.

Action Plan

Select Businesses

- Choose businesses that align with the wants and needs of the people in your network, such as career consultants, real estate agents, health clubs, etc.

Identify Ideal Customers

- If your personal network isn't extensive enough for referrals, start identifying the ideal customers for the businesses you want to collaborate with.

Understand the Customer Profile

- Like the person specification section in a job description, create a detailed profile of your ideal customer. This should include demographics, social habits, and behavioral traits.
- Start by answering specific questions to get a clear picture:
  - Age, location, gender
  - Race, income level, homeowner status
  - Education, occupation, family status
  - Content preferences (audio, video, written)
  - Favorite websites, apps, interests, hobbies

Explore DistroList.app

- Put those answers into the DistroList.app to discover the people, places, and things that already speak to your target audience.

Step 4: Signpost Them

Your signposts are essentially your ads that direct your ideal customers to the businesses you have an agreement with. So for your signposts to have any effect, you want them in places where your ideal customers will see them.

To do that, you typically have 3 options – become a content creator, become an online marketer, or tap someone else's network.

Option 1: Become a Content Creator

This is where you build your own audience of potential buyers on one or more social platforms (Facebook, Instagram, TikTok). You would be stepping into the shoes of a content creator in hopes of building a fanbase which, over time, you will expect to have a degree of influence over. If you build up a highly engaged audience, you'd be well positioned to serve them recommendations on products or services with the businesses you have agreements with.

However, for that to work, it would require that your audience be aligned with the businesses you represent. For example, promoting home-delivered steaks to an audience full of vegans and animal-cruelty activists would be a mistake. This is where you go back to *who* your ideal customer is and start creating content for that persona.

To begin to attract this audience, you could write blogs, create a daily podcast, make vlogs, create YouTube videos, write books, or host seminars and online webinars. The options are constantly growing, so choose the one you feel most comfortable with and start creating content to attract the eyes and ears of the people you can then promote an offer to.

Does this option sound right for you?

Your answer should be NO. It shouldn't sound right at all. It's way too slow. Sure, it's a great long-term strategy, but that's not what this recipe is about. To start making money immediately, you need a faster, more agile way to get your offer in front of your ideal customers.

Let's move on to the next option!

Option 2: Become an Online Marketer

This is where you take it several steps further and force results by paying for advertisements you hope will drive buyers to your offer.

You want to create an advertisement designed to grab your ideal customer's attention. To do that, you need to learn how to use ad managers to create and control those promotions. Then, you'll need to learn how to design those ads to fit the ad specifications of the platform(s) you decide to advertise on. You could create sponsored posts on Facebook and Instagram, through display ads, email marketing, and writing all the ad copy yourself. You may even take it a step further and start creating marketing funnels, where you make a series of web pages tailor-made to increase your sales conversions.

That's one side of the job. The other part is finding out where to put those ads. This is where you look at the types of businesses you have collaborated with, figure out who your ideal customers are, and find out where they go online. Once you determine that, you simply go and buy ad space and promote there.

Sounds like a plan, right?

Yeah, sure… it's technically a sound plan, but it's also filled with holes. Creating ads and working with ad managers is complex stuff. They are fiddly as hell, and when you start allocating ad spend budgets, you could very well see your money disappearing faster than you'd like. Of course, there is a right way to do it, and for that, you'll need a professional… and a big budget.

Then, on top of that, even though your ideal customers are seeing your ad, why would they click on it? What? Because you made a pretty ad? Because you used a fancy meme with some clever wordplay to create a great piece of clickbait? That might get you the click, but it in no way promises a sale. And then, there's a trust component you are missing because they just don't know you…

Again, this is not going to work for us. While it is a fast way to get your offers in front of your ideal customers, it's complex and hard to do correctly. We don't have time for something complex and hard to do right now. Let's go to option 3.

Option 3: Tap Someone Else's Network

This option is by far the fastest way to get you started at a low-to-no upfront cost to you. Your job here is to tap into the network of someone who has already gathered your ideal customers. You're going to have them do the marketing for you.

If you've been following this recipe, you should have come to an agreement with a local small-to-medium business, right? The strategy I'm about to share with you is focused on how you can make money with small to medium businesses. If you don't know what I'm talking about, go back to step 1.

> ### Pro Tip
>
> To get the word out, start tapping into influencer audiences to leverage their reach and credibility to your advantage. Don't forget to look into partnerships with other companies so that you can make use of their existing customer bases, too. By remembering both these strategies, you'll maximize your exposure and profitability with little-to-no upfront costs.

There are 2 strategies you can go with – tap influencer audiences or tap another company's customers – and both of these address the trust component I just mentioned. I recommend cycling through both strategies periodically for the best results.

Strategy 1: Tapping Influencer Audiences

Influencers range from small bloggers with just a few hundred followers to those with a massive following in the millions, giving them a celebrity-like status that we see every day. They exist in every market, no matter which industry or niche your business sits in. The best part is that they can sway the buying decisions of their audience, meaning your goal is to collaborate with influencers whose audience is filled with your ideal customers.

Before we begin, I want you to be realistic about what we are doing here. So much goes into putting together a well-thought-out influencer marketing campaign. But this is not that kind of campaign. This is all about following the path of least resistance to get the immediate results you need. We'll get into more structured approaches later on.

To start, I want you to look for influencers local to your business with between 1,000 and 10,000 followers. The ones with smaller follower counts tend to have a more personal relationship with their followers. They tend to be your normal everyday person who only just started experimenting with the idea of sponsored content, like a paid shoutout here and there. At this stage, for them, influencer marketing is definitely not a full-time job or primary income stream.

These influencers are great to work with, especially when you're starting a new business with a small marketing budget. They're inexpensive, more authentic, relatable, and approachable, and therefore, they have closer relationships with their community and higher engagement rates.

Working with them is much less expensive and sometimes even free, meaning the lower upfront costs allow you to work with multiple influencers at the same time. You'll find that this group is much easier to work with, very agreeable with contract terms, and best of all, they are easy to recruit. So, let's go find them!

Here are 3 quick ways to find the ones who have enough of your ideal customers in their audience:

1. This is where we **use these keywords and interests as hashtags to search social platforms for influencers that match the brand**. Most social media platforms have search functions, meaning you can research categories, hashtags, and keywords that will pull up closely matching content creators. Searching social platforms like this will usually pull up influencers with huge follower numbers. Contacting those influencers may be a bit too ambitious at this early stage. Take the time to dig deeper to find those within the range you need (1,000 to 10,000 followers). One shortcut that has served me well is the "follower the follower" hack. People who become influencers tend to be inspired by other big influencers out there. So by searching their followers, you can find smaller versions of them that fit the follower count range you're looking for.

2. **Look at the social accounts of the business you're engaged with.** If they have an active social media presence, you could look at the people who already follow them. You may find people who are already raving fans of that business and would love to work with you. Because you didn't find these people using the keywords, interests, and

hashtags you created, you may get a welcome side effect. This group of people will offer you a different, untapped audience with potentially better engagement rates and better prices.

3. I created an app, DistroList.app, **which you can use to search for influencers based on location, number of followers, gender, and interests**. You can also find influencers whose audience matches the demographics and interests of your ideal customer. You can even filter these results by audience size and engagement rates to help you find your match. We have also built in some powerful tools to help you streamline your outreach so that you can connect and collaborate with your partners faster. We're adding new features all the time, and you can try it for free. www.distrolist.app

These search techniques should be enough to get you going. As you progress through this book, you'll learn even more techniques and hacks that made my business go from making thousands to millions.

To help ensure the influencer and my brand are compatible, I ask myself the following questions:

Q1: Are there enough of my ideal customers in their audience?

Because your goal is to generate sales from members of their audience, it's important to make sure that the audience represents a large enough number of your ideal customers. Answering this question ensures that your influencer marketing campaign has a chance of being profitable.

Remember, anyone with a large audience can be considered an influencer since it's commonly accepted that popularity and influence go hand-in-hand. So, don't fall into the trap of thinking that high follower numbers guarantee high levels of engagement and more sales.

Q2: Does the influencer publish content around themes that resonate with my brand?

If the influencer publishes content that shares similar themes with your brand, it will be much easier for you to create value and deliver a sales message in an insightful and engaging way. You are essentially trying to connect your brand with the brand identity the influencer has created for themselves.

For example, influencers who keep the content they publish rotating around a handful of categories tend to give their followers a better understanding of who they are and what they are about. That usually makes for a much better-connected audience and gives them a well-rounded and easily recognizable brand.

Q3: Does the influencer have enough influence to carry my sales message?

You want to know if the influencer has built up a relationship with your ideal customers because we know that what makes an influencer "good" or "valuable" is based on whether they can keep people engaged for a long time. So, you want to know what type of dialogue the influencer has with their audience and whether they have the "trust" and "authority" to carry your sales message.

A good indicator of how influential an influencer can be for your campaign is to look at their level of engagement. That means looking at the number of likes, comments, and shares an influencer receives per post. An easy way to do this is to look at their last three posts to get an initial idea, but there are better ways to evaluate engagement.

There are a few simple calculations for different social media platforms that give you an engagement score.

(Total Engagement / Total Followers) x 100 = Engagement Rate

Note: There is no official engagement rate formula, but they generally revolve around this central equation.

However, these formulas can be enhanced to factor in many more data points that can lead to even more complex, multi-platform equations. Generally speaking, a higher score is usually better.

On top of that, there's also a growing number of apps that can be used to discover and evaluate influencers, including DistroList.app.

Q4: Can I serve the audience in a non-competitive but profitable way for the both of us?

Most influencers work with multiple brands to make a living, meaning they may already be promoting similar products to yours. This can be the case with smaller follower counts, too. Since these influencers are starting to monetize their audience with aligned brands, it's best to take a quick look at their social media profiles and recent posts to see if they are promoting any products or brands that directly compare with yours. Sometimes, a glance like that highlights any obvious signs of competing interests or other contractual obligations already in place that may restrict them from working with you.

I suggest going through these quick qualifying questions with every influencer you consider so that you don't waste time or money working with someone who can't help you. Influencers who say they're interested would naturally want to know what's in it for them. Just like when you approached those businesses initially, if you leave it up to them to set the terms, they'll get way too creative.

So, to avoid all that, be ready with an offer they can either accept or not. How will you incentivize them to promote for you? You could pay the influencer a flat one-time fee to promote your offer, or you could take the deal you have and offer to cut them in.

Model 1: Paying a One-Time Fee

This is one of the most popular ways to start because you can very easily control your financial exposure. No matter the content type (text, video, picture, live stream), you only pay a flat rate. You can even negotiate a flat fee for a larger campaign where the influencer posts content in different formats on multiple social media platforms at predefined dates and times. And if they don't work out, you can simply not use them again.

Having said that, I want to give you some guidelines to follow when working with influencers. Whether you're working with someone who has 1,000 followers, 10,000 followers, 100,000 followers, or even 1M followers, there are lots of other things to consider regarding how much you could (or should) pay out for an influencer promotion.

When you first start discussing what you want from the influencer, like with any job description, they will want to know what is expected of them. You must be specific. Define, even spell out specific talking points to include in the promotion, including what not to say. Tell them what format you want that shoutout created in (text, picture, video, live stream) and which social channels you want it on.

You need to be that specific to get what you want from them and control your financial exposure while maximizing what you can gain from this collaboration.

However, I should warn you that the more you ask for, the more expensive it will get. In fact, a few things can affect pricing, and while I don't want to side-track and dive too deep into influencer pricing dynamics, I want to make you aware of some of the main ones.

#1: Content Format and Social Channels

Platforms allow influencers to create a variety of content like photos, videos, live streams, and blogs. So, when you consider the price of a one-time, pay-per-post pricing style, an influencer may have a higher price for a video post and a lower price for uploading a photo.

Also, your influencers often have a presence across multiple platforms, and your audience will more than likely use more than one social media network. For that reason, cross-platform promotions are a great way to give your audience various ways to engage with business. Cross-platform posting also factors in the different formats and, therefore, the work, time, and resources the post requires. The more you want, the more expensive it can get.

#2: Production Costs

Do you require the influencer to produce a high-quality video? How much content are you going to ask them to create? Do they have to travel to a location or attend an event to create the post?

The more it costs the influencer to create the content you want, the more you can be expected to pay. So when you're starting out, can you make do with less than the higher quality? It can be tempting to ask for nicer-looking content and more posts. However, remember that off-the-cuff influencer content tends to give off a higher sense of authenticity. Think about what made influencers attractive in the first place.

#3: The Price of Your Product or Service

The price of your product or service, coupled with the type of target audience, will also impact how much you pay. For example, if your company sells seats in private jet charters, you must find influencers who communicate with that audience.

This means your pricing would be in line with the buying power of that audience. To put it differently, influencers who target higher-earning audiences typically charge more for promotions. So, the more expensive the product or service, the higher the cost will likely be too.

#4: Industry or Category

A wide variety of audience interests exists, so there are a lot of industries and categories in which influencers serve and specialize in. Each has different types of influencers, content delivery styles, audiences, and competition that all affect how much they charge.

For example, in popular markets like fitness, fashion, and beauty, you will probably have a lot more influencers who make their category more competitive and, therefore, cheaper. But in less popular areas like technology, business strategy, and finance, it could be more expensive because the influencer's knowledge and expertise around that topic is harder to come by.

#5: Agency Representation

Lots of influencers in the world have made influencer marketing their full-time career, or at least have an ambition to make it so. Because of that, you'll see that it's not uncommon to find many of the influencers partnered with agencies that help them find better opportunities. It's similar to how people sign up with recruitment firms or talent agencies to look for jobs. If you find an influencer partnered with an agency, you'll need to contact the agency to work with them.

Influencers represented by agencies tend to be more professional and have larger followers with higher engagement rates with their audiences. Since you're starting out, it will be more cost-effective to work with unrepresented influencers initially.

#6: Reuse and Licensing

Will you want to reshare, reuse, or repurpose a piece of content you pay an influencer to post? You may want to repost the content on your own social media channels or perhaps repurpose it for different types of advertising, like display ads, testimonial pages, and other forms of advertising.

Some influencers may want to charge additional licensing fees to reuse any content they create for you. If you do, have it agreed upon in writing.

#7: Seasonality and Demand

Advertising with influencers is similar to advertising anywhere else. If you want them to promote around religious holidays, seasonal holidays, and new year promotions, expect to pay more. If there is a higher demand, you will pay higher prices.

#8: Exclusivity

You might want your influencer to promote your content exclusively, which can be valuable but also expensive. If you go for this option, you'll be limiting or eliminating the influencer's other potential income opportunities, meaning a higher cost to you.

Model 2: Cutting Them In

This is where you offer the influencer a share of the profit you would be making. What I love most about this model is that you will pay an influencer when they give you a paying customer. Personally, I prefer performance-based partnerships when dealing with higher price points because percentage splits will hold a higher value for the influencer. With larger amounts of money involved, the larger the commission they can earn.

For example, let's say you negotiated a 20% commission on all sales at a luxury watch store when your referrals buy. In this case, you could offer 15% of the sale to an influencer who can land you a customer.

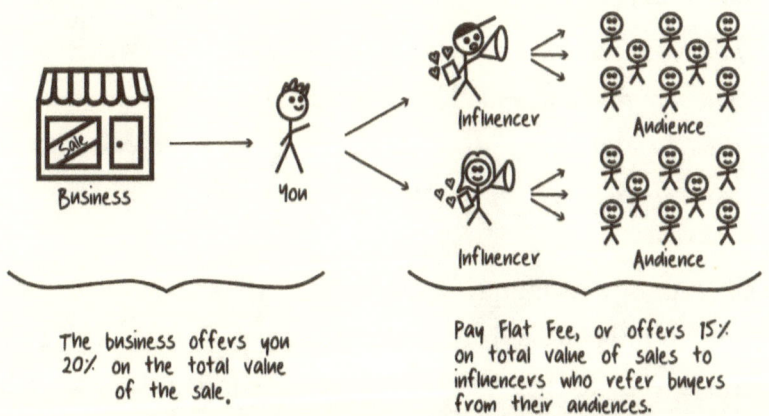

The business offers you 20% on the total value of the sale.

Pay flat fee, or offers 15% on total value of sales to influencers who refer buyers from their audiences.

To do this, you need to give these influencers a unique identifier to track the referrals. For example, you could have a coupon code, promo code, or affiliate link that tracks a paying referral back to the influencer who made the promotion.

This is a crucial component because:

a. The business you're engaged with will know that the referral came from your network, so they reward you and

b. You know which influencer in your network actually referred that particular buyer so that you can reward them.

Once you've found some potential influencers to partner with, to get things started, simply reach out and ask them if they'd be interested. It's almost the same way you made contact with the businesses you initially reached out to. Contacting an influencer is as easy as looking them up on social media (preferably the platform they use most of the time) and sending them a direct message (DM).

You could write something like:

> *Hi, I've been following your content and love your posts about [Topic/Products]. I represent [Business]. We have a similar audience to yours, and I'd love to talk to you about sponsored posts / a joint venture promotion. Are you available for a quick chat this week? I'm available at [Contact Info].*

Also, if your offer is unique or exclusive to you, it will make it more difficult for influencers or members of their audience to go around you and directly to the business you partnered with. This could be a unique product or service that only you are promoting. Therefore, all sales of that offer must filter through you and your network.

Unless the business you partner with has an affiliate platform set up for you, the quickest and easiest way to get started is to set up unique promo codes you give your influencers. Each influencer would get their own unique code to promote with.

Strategy 2: Tapping Another Company's Customers

I spoke about how to leverage other people's audiences in the first strategy. This one is about how to leverage other people's products. It's a timeless strategy and always gets me results.

I want you to think about which products and services people are using that complement the one you're promoting. The reason for this is that those other products will target similar customer demographics as your ideal customer, meaning (much like how it is with influencers) they will have some influence over their customers. They can also contact their customer base directly at any time they want.

However, unlike influencer audiences, these businesses have already sold something, within your market and niche, to their customer base. That makes their customer list warmer, with potentially lots of buyers waiting for your offer. These buyers don't know you, but they are looking for solutions in your market, and they've made purchases with businesses whose products or services complement your own. Their relationship with their customers is something you can leverage in a way that is profitable for both businesses. Getting one of these businesses to promote your offer for you is one of the easiest ways to get some quick sales through the door.

This is where a joint venture partnership (JV) works well. Since those businesses already have a relationship with their customers, they can endorse your offer, and in doing so, they lend you their credibility. As a result, their customers may feel more comfortable checking out your offer.

These JV promotions can be extremely simple, too. Have you ever purchased something you received in the mail that also had flyers with other things inside it? In fact, look at your email inbox, and you'll likely find a lot of promotional emails from businesses you know doing the same thing.

I can't emphasize enough how useful this strategy is when you're starting out. One simple message endorsing your offer can pull in a lot of sales very, very quickly.

Contacting businesses for this type of partnership differs from contacting small influencers with follower counts of between 1,000 and 10,000. The products and services that complement the business you represent will likely include national well-known brands as well as local smaller and private ones.

With this in mind, when looking for businesses to partner with, I usually look for a private company, preferably local to the one I represent. If it's an online business where location isn't a factor, I look for someone who has created their own brand and built their own customer list from scratch. These people and businesses are more likely to be receptive and open to a conversation about being paid to endorse my products or services.

Let me show you two easy techniques to find these businesses – manual search and Similarweb.

#1: Manual Search

I want you to consider all the products and services people use before, during, and after the one you represent. For example, let's say you represent a health club, and broadly speaking, your ideal customer is someone who wants to get in shape. Joining your club is only one part of your customer's journey to getting in shape since they will need many other products and services to meet their health goals.

Your job is to find all these other products and services and try to tap into their customer lists. In this example, you could find books, blogs, and websites promoting a special diet. There could be new specialty clothing brands for sports apparel, or there could be home equipment, a nutritionist, private personal trainers, physiotherapists, and anything else that people use before, during, or after working out at the gym.

An easy way to kick start this process is to use ChatGPT or any other equivalent AI platform to quickly list the types of products and services that people would use. You could create a prompt as simple as "Can you give me a list of the products and services people use before, during, and after [Insert Product]." Currently, ChatGPT and the other LLMs out there like Google Gemini (formerly Bard) could create a list of the *types* of products and services and even crawl the internet for you. This initial list is a great starting point, but I still recommend manually searching Google to build on that list.

If you took the time to understand who your customer is, you will know what solutions they're looking for and where they are looking for them. Find out what they are buying before, during, and after they use your product, and you'll know whose customer list you want to leverage. Go ahead and start making your list of businesses.

#2: Similarweb

With our goal to find out what people are buying before and after using the thing you're selling, I also recommend using Similarweb. It's a really helpful platform because you can put in any business' URL, and it will tell you who the competitors are for that site. It does that by showing you where else people go based on their own searches for solutions to problems they have. This information is available under the "Competitors" tab. It shows you a list of websites that are in the same industry as the website you entered and have a similar traffic profile.

Among a host of other options, the platform also provides information about website traffic, such as where it is coming from, where it is going to, and who your visitors are. For example, they have a tab for "Audience Insights," which provides information about a website's visitors, such as their demographics, interests, and online behavior. There's also a slew of other analytics and data you can look into, but it can get quite complex, so please don't get lost in there!

Go to the site (there should be a free trial), type in a URL, and see which sites directly compete with the website you entered. If any of them look good, add them to your list.

Reach Out

There are many more ways to find people and businesses with audiences and customer lists that will be valuable to you. I'll get into that later in this book. Right now, I'm providing guerilla warfare tactics to get some immediate results.

The next step is reaching out to them, and just as you've kept things short and sweet before, it's no different now.

You can send an email saying something like this:

> *Hi [Prospect's Name],*
>
> *My name is [Your Name], and I represent [Company]. We share a similar consumer group, and we would like to connect with you to discuss the possibility of working together on a joint venture.*

If you are open to a conversation, I'd like to set up a call this week to discuss a collaboration that would be profitable and bring value to both our companies.

Kind regards,
[Your Name]

These emails should be easy to read and fast to scan. You can get into the juicer details when they respond.

Also, this email template can be used as a telephone opener script or even a direct message on social media. I really want you to get used to firing these opener scripts off the hip. You'll be surprised at how often they will hit and open doors for you. But for them to work, you need a list of targets and be constantly firing away.

Pro Tip

Always remember, you are never acting alone. When reaching out to potential collaborators and partners, focus on how you both benefit. Joint ventures like this are usually win-win situations, so don't hesitate to emphasize that point up front. To increase your chances of success, use AI language model apps like ChatGPT to easily generate different outreach templates. This can save you a lot of time and effort when crafting personalized messages while still maintaining a professional and effective tone.

Moving on. The next thing you need to have prepared is the one question everyone who agrees to talk will want answered – how it will be profitable for them. Obvious, right?

In much the same way you had those two options on the table for influencers, it's the same here – one-off fee or cut them in on the deal.

Model 1: One-Off Fee

This is where you pay a one-off fee for a company to send a simple message to endorse your offer. An endorsement could be communicated in any format they use to engage with their customers. It could be a direct email to all their customers or a multi-touch campaign using a combination of formats like direct mail, email, text message blasts, and even social media posts.

However, before you agree to anything, when you discuss the available options, be crystal clear about one super-crucial thing. When they communicate your brand to their customers, the promotion needs to be all about your brand. Don't waste your time if they try to mix you into other stuff they are marketing.

Think of this the same as how you would pay an influencer for a shoutout. You are offering to pay them to make a post endorsing you and only you.

Also, make sure they are not spamming their customers already. That's no good for anyone. If they are, their customers will probably ignore their marketing attempts, meaning you'd be throwing your money away.

Ask them 3 simple questions to avoid falling into that trap:

1. What did they send out in their last 3-5 mailouts, emails, texts, and social posts?
2. How many customers do they actually have, preferably for the products or services relevant to your business? The bigger, the better, obviously.
3. What are their engagement numbers on the format they intend to endorse you on? This means you want to know how many people opened their emails, how many were read, how many responded to text campaigns, how many commented on social media posts, and so on.

This information will help you decide if you want to work with them. You can guesstimate whether they'll be able to drive in a decent amount of sales and help you work out a one-time promotional fee you'll be happy with.

A simple way to do this is to look at how much money you make per sale and then at how much engagement you can expect. Admittedly, at this point, you'll be flat-out guessing because you don't have any sales and conversion rates (from ads you've run) to work from.

If you followed this recipe, have a product or service that pays out a healthy margin, and the business you want to partner with has good engagement numbers, you're in a good spot. For now, just try to negotiate the lowest price possible to minimize your risk. We'll get to sales page conversion rates later.

And when it comes to pricing, those bigger and more established companies are more than likely experienced with this strategy. They'll probably have a readymade media kit that lists their options and prices. This is where it can get very expensive very quickly, so I urge you to focus on smaller private brands.

I wish I could give you a set pricing structure that you'll typically pay, but it will always be a negotiation. But remember this, the advantage of paying a one-time fee is that you will get immediate results, meaning you'll either benefit from a nice influx of new sales or you can cut your losses if you get a flat response.

Model 2: Cutting Them In

Instead of doing a promotion where the business would promote my offer to their customer only once, this marketing technique makes it evergreen.

The plan here is to integrate your products and services. They call this promotion customer integration marketing – and it's been one of my secret weapons for a long, long time.

Having said that, this integrated effort is not actually a secret. In fact, marketing channel integration has been around for a long time. It's where businesses combine and promote different products or services together to create more value for their customers and increase sales for the businesses involved. Instead of promoting each product separately, they show how using multiple products together can enhance the overall customer experience. Essentially, they consider what they can offer that complements their initial offer and has enough sales potential for the collaboration to be profitable.

Sometimes, these promotions can be so seamless that a customer may not know where the business activities from one business ends and when those of another begin. But when you see it in action, it's usually the bigger companies doing it, *not* the startup entrepreneurs who could really benefit from it when starting out.

I personally think every business should have a strategy for integrating their offers with marketing other complementary products and services. It quite literally works with any product or service out there, and it's a continuous promotional effort that can bring value to both businesses – not a one-time promotion.

Let me share a quick example with you. I partnered with a high-end jewelry store that specialized in luxury watches and worked out a 30% commission on the total value of sales I would bring them.

I remember contacting many boutique investment firms in London that sold alternative investments, such as fine art, fine wine, precious gems, and rare earth metals. I knew they had wealthy clients who might consider treating themselves to a luxury watch after they make their investment in fine art.

So, whenever an investor buys a collectible Warhol or Banksy painting, they receive a special offer to buy a luxury watch to celebrate the moment.

Hey, when buying a $400,000 painting, you might be in the mood to treat yourself to a $40,000 special-edition, super-rare Rolex!

I remember giving the fine art boutique a 20% commission, which meant I was left with 10% of the 30% total. And in doing so, I successfully integrated the high-end jewelry store's products with the fine art investment boutiques.

When a sale was made, everyone won. The jewelry store scored a sale, made a profit, and got a new customer, who would likely become a repeat customer. I benefited in the same way, with a modest 10% commission, and the fine art boutique received 20%. They had simply served their customer with an offer that complements their purchase in a non-competitive way for both businesses involved.

This pairing goes both ways. It can be reversed, too. Customers from the high-end jewelry store might be interested in learning about fine art investments. So, of course, I reversed the deal, too! Both companies pool each other's customers, maximizing the value they can offer and extract.

Imagine selling a single watch at a price point of $10,000. My commissions would have been 30%, $3,000. But I offered the fine art boutique 20% of the total sale, $2,000, and I was left with 10% at $1,000.

Now, reverse the deal and run the same commission splits with the fine art investment example at $400,000. Imagine you brought in a buyer through the jewelry store, where the store earned 20% commission, and you earned 10%. That's a $40,000 commission payable to you. Crazy, right? It's like making money out of nothing!

Everyone wins here. All you need to do is look for businesses whose products or services complement yours. You can look for the things people buy before, during, or after they make these types of purchases. Or look into which substitute products they are buying instead of the product you represent. Look at what else they are spending the same type of money on that are not competitors.

Once you have your list, all you need to do is reach out to them and present the collaboration idea. If they agree, you'll have a near-endless supply of free customers. It will literally run for as long as your collaboration is in place.

It's so, so, so much more effective than the one-time promotion since your offer is being presented to your target customers every time they buy.

The easiest way to set this up is with a promo code, coupon, or voucher. The business you represent could provide you with a special offer, such as a 10% discount voucher (exclusive to you) on any purchase over $10,000. All the customers that use the promo code are immediately linked to you and the company you integrated the offer with.

By the way, the promotion could be as simple as sending a flyer to a buyer along with whatever they purchased. Or, it could be a promotion sent along with an email receipt. You could embed the promotion in that company's online sales funnel, where the offer is presented as an upsell or even a down-sell. It might even be physically presented by an in-person salesperson, as with my fine art boutique.

Do you see how simple this is? Think about how you could scale it up. If you reached out to 100 businesses and only 20% agreed, that would mean you'd have 20 businesses selling your product or service to their own customers.

I hope you can see how incredibly powerful that is. Suppose you have 20 businesses that agree to promote for you. That's like having 20 super-elite salespeople selling your stuff to warm customers they already have a relationship with, and you only pay them if they make a sale.

If you built that list and started contacting them all, and we factor in time for negotiations, callbacks, and rejections, you could easily average ONE signup per week. In 3 months, you could have 12 businesses promoting for you. It's like printing money.

This strategy, by itself, could be all you need to go from zero to hero. And if I'm being perfectly honest with you, it is the actual cornerstone of my own money-making journey. Without mastering this marketing technique, I would have never made the money I did. You can apply this process over and over so that you can create so much demand, and sell so fast, that your biggest problem will be making sure you have enough supply!

In Part 1, we focused on helping you generate immediate income to meet your financial needs, and now, we're shifting gears to Part 2: Create Irresistible Offers, On Demand. This section is all about equipping you with the tools to build a profitable and sustainable business. This is an easy-to-learn, tried-and-tested recipe for creating a successful business right from the word go.

Action Plan

Option 1: Becoming a Content Creator

- Build an audience on social platforms like Facebook, Instagram, and TikTok.
- Create content tailored to your ideal customer.

*** Recognize this as a long-term strategy that is not suitable for immediate results.

Option 2: Becoming an Online Marketer

- Design advertisements to capture the attention of your ideal customers.
- Learn to use ad managers for creating and controlling promotions.
- Determine where to place ads based on the business type and customer profile.

*** Understand the complexity and financial implications of this approach.

Option 3: Tapping Someone Else's Network

- Use other people's networks who have already gathered your ideal customers.
- Focus on small-to-medium businesses for partnerships.

*** Remember, this method offers a faster, low-to-no upfront cost approach.

Strategy 1: Tapping Influencer Audiences

- Collaborate with influencers whose audience matches your ideal customers.

- Consider targeting influencers with 1,000 to 10,000 followers for authenticity and higher engagement.

- Use social media and DistroList.app to find suitable influencers.

- Ensure influencers align with your brand and have enough influence.

- Consider the influencer's content format, production costs, and industry when determining compensation.

- Offer a one-time fee or a commission on sales for influencer collaborations.

Strategy 2: Tapping Another Company's Customers

- Identify products and services complementary to what you're promoting.

- Leverage joint venture partnerships for promoting offers.

- Use manual searches and tools like Similarweb to find complementary businesses.

- Reach out to potential businesses with a clear and concise message.

- Opt for either a one-off fee or a commission-based model for the partnership.

- Integrate marketing efforts for continuous promotion, not just one-time events.

Part 2

CREATE IRRESISTIBLE OFFERS, ON DEMAND

"Develop your own offer, which people actually want, at the exact time they want it"

What Do I Actually Do?

"So, what do you do," she asked.

Her eyes were sparkling in the low lights of the bar we were in. She smiled attractively as she sipped her cocktail. She was holding my gaze. Expectantly. Awaiting my response. She was interested. She was curious. I was on a date, and in that moment, I was lost for words. I was drawing a blank. Actually, no, it wasn't a blank... it was information overload. My mind was flooded with too many options as answers to her question.

I was frozen in thought.

At first, I thought I could tell her I worked in the finance sector as an investment broker. But no, I couldn't say that because it's not exactly true. A few probing questions would quickly reveal that I didn't know anything about finance and that all I really did was promote investment opportunities through distribution channels.

So, then I figured I should just tell her I'm a marketer. Ah, but no. I can't say that because I'd be selling myself short. I collaborate with companies on a much deeper level than that.

Okay then, what about saying I'm a consultant? But that's too vague and kind of boring. Definitely, don't be boring. Boring is bad.

I could say I run a consultancy that goes beyond advertising, branding, and direct response campaigns in that we also cultivate distribution channels that connect our clients to people and other businesses within their respective markets, driving up sales with targeted buyer groups. No, I can't say that. This is not *that* kind of a sales pitch. However, I was definitely trying to sell myself. In any case, if I say that, I would be leaving out all the other businesses I'm involved with.

I'd be leaving out so much. What about telling her about the training and coaching business I had? Or the online Software as a Service (SaaS) I created. Or the chocolate bars I was manufacturing.

Okay, this is getting too messy now, I thought. Argh, why don't I just tell her I'm an entrepreneur? Nah, that's too cheesy. Fine then, screw it. I'll just tell her I'm an opportunist, kind of like a pirate from kid stories. Just show me the recipe for making money, which is kind of like giving me a treasure map, and I'll scramble together a crew and find a ship to go and find that gold… no, that's a weird analogy, and it's way too honest!

By this point, with my mind going through all these options, I had run out of time. Too much time had passed. She had watched me "on pause," staring directly back at her but also somehow staring into space, glassy-eyed and stuck cycling through all those options. Anything I said now would probably sound like I'd just made it up.

So, in a desperate attempt to save face and change the subject, I said, "What is this, a job interview? I thought we were on a date. Don't you like my dashing good looks?" Yeah, that was smart and witty, I thought. Good job brain!

But it didn't work. I had stalled too long. Now she was really curious. She said (in a comically, somewhat condescending tone, but somehow still managing to stay cute), "What? Haha, nice try. What are you, a secret agent or something?"

I caved at this point and went on to explain all the businesses I was involved in. I was breaking a cardinal rule of dating in that I was making the conversation about me, me, me. This date was doomed.

My sudden stage fright was because I had my hands in more than a few cookie jars. At that point, I was selling real estate, diamonds, and gold under my brand Core Assets. I had a recruitment business, Core Agents, specializing in sales staff and later matching businesses with businesses. I had a training and coaching company, Core Training, where government contracts paid me to provide career advice and teach entry-level employability-related work skills to the long-term unemployed. I had an online SaaS that was a business directory, Core Index, which gave the subscriber the "who's who" with corporate executives in the UK and provided their direct emails and telephone lines. That business barely had a chance to get off the ground because, around the same time, LinkedIn really took off and dominated that space. I even joint ventured into a London-based candy shop chain and co-created a chocolate bar, Yummy Bar. Funny enough, I was tempted to call the chocolate bar Core Bar, in keeping with naming all my businesses beginning with the word Core. However, Core Bar sounded more suited to a fitness-focused protein bar. The chocolate bar I was manufacturing was intended to be more… yummy. Hence, Core Bar being shelved, and Yummy Bar prevailing.

I stopped there, but as crazy as it may sound, there were other businesses, too. At first, my date looked as if she was impressed. But then, she said on second thought that my business and work life must be very intense and demanding. She then went on to state the obvious in that I probably don't have much of a life outside of work, and this date would be out of my normal routine, which it was. She also thought I might have an identity crisis and perhaps be a jack of all trades! If you think she sounds like a shrink, you'd be correct. She was actually a couples therapist by profession.

However, in my defense, and I'm no expert here, but being on the defensive on your first date with someone is probably another bad spot to be in. I said I had heard somewhere that to be happy and successful, you should stick to your passions, follow your heart, and choose a job doing whatever interests you most.

As we all know, the real world is more than a little harsh. It's unrealistic to think you can simply land a job at the drop of a hat in any industry you want.

But I had found that I could explore my interests and earn money at the same time by creating businesses as collaborations or joint ventures with already established brands in the market I wanted to be involved with. I had admittedly taken it a little too far and become a bit of a startup junkie. The more I thought about it, the more befitting the label of being a jack of all trades and master of none sounded.

I could step into almost any business sector I wanted and benefit by making money while satisfying my curiosity and interests. If I wanted to be involved with real estate investments, I could collaborate with a property developer and refer them to real estate investors. If I wanted to be involved with fintech software, media, and even street-facing businesses like restaurants, nightclubs, and jewelry stores, I could. I was even involved with companies mining rare earth metals and precious gems through to the production of rubber, targeting companies manufacturing shoe soles.

I'd simply find the companies in those markets, find out who their customers/buyers are, and get in between and negotiate a fee.

My collaborations were becoming more complex, too. With some companies, I found myself so deeply embedded in their operations and supply chains that I had transcended from simple referral or introducer agreements to increasingly more complex joint ventures and strategic partnerships.

In the end, I conceded. I agreed my business was quite an overwhelming way to operate. It was messy, disorganized, and very hard to manage.

A few weeks later, I was having drinks with my friend, Matt, and I remember telling him about that "date" and joking about how that night had somehow turned into an intervention for me and ended up being the wake-up call I needed.

Side note: That date had not gone as badly as I initially thought. That beautiful woman I was having drinks with is now my wife, Erika, and the mother of my daughters, Valentina and Sofia.

Creating My Own Niche

I realized it was time I stopped experimenting with different markets and focused, choosing one market, creating my own niche, building one brand, and scaling it up.

While I had figured out how to *try out* being in business in different markets and make a good amount of money while doing so, I did not truly know what the target audience in these markets really wanted. The issue was that I was collaborating with companies that were the experts in their markets, assuming they knew their business. I was not the expert. I was only partnering with them and signposting their targeted buyers in their direction for a fee.

Whenever I thought about carving out my own niche by choosing one market and coming up with a compelling offer of my own, I went around in circles in an endless loop of options. Mostly, I caught myself creating another me-too niche. I was worried about choosing a fad that would fizzle out, picking a market with too many competitors, or selecting something no one wanted. It was analysis paralysis.

My big mistake was looking at niche markets and trying to build a business around one I liked. This is wrong, and it's a mistake many other entrepreneurs make, too. The entire point of finding your niche is to sell to an audience without lots of competitors coming after your customers. By choosing an existing niche, you chase the same customers with the same solutions as someone else. You are increasing the competition in that marketplace and competing for the same customers.

The questions that hammered my mind like a never-ending migraine were:

- What would make my offer unique?
- What would set me apart?
- How is it possible for *me* to create a niche?
- If I thought I created a niche offer, how would I know if the people in my chosen market would like it?
- Could I sell enough of whatever it was and make enough money?

Matt worked at a financial services firm in London, and he gave me a tip for how firms could create a brand new financial product and have it make millions of dollars, almost as soon as they launch the offer. In fact, they had a rule that with whatever new offer they launched, they aimed to break even within their first week. They would even have internal competitions on whether a department could break even in under 24 hours!

Everything from that point forward was pure profit. What he said next, in an instant, provided a solution to my analysis paralysis. It had me seeing clearly again. It was such a simple thing, too. It wasn't a new groundbreaking strategy or something super complex, either. It was simply looking at the problem through a different lens. And when I looked through this new lens, everything became clear.

Learning From Someone Who's Done It

He said, "Sav, mate, no wonder you're pulling your hair out. You're going about this all wrong. You're guessing, and that's your problem. You need to find out what the clients want. That will tell you which direction to go with your offer."

Not surprisingly, I promptly replied, "No shit, Sherlock. I know that. Everybody knows that. The question is, how do I find out what they want with the resources I have? I'm not a fancy financial firm like the company you work for. I don't have a market research or internal product development department at my disposal."

He responded, "Easy, all you have to do is literally ask your clients what questions they have about your submarket. That will tell you what they want and need so that you can find or create a solution to sell them. It works just as well with warm leads if you don't have a big enough client list. It's a simple survey, mate. Not magic. We do it all the time, and the next round of beers is on you."

I would have probably bought him whatever he wanted at that moment! What he told me was so simple, yet so powerful.

Matt went on to explain that when the firm he worked for ran out of things to sell their clients (he actually put it in financial lingo – when their investment products were fully subscribed), they would send out surveys to all their clients and email lists, literally asking them what they want.

These surveys were sent out under the guise of customer satisfaction surveys, asking them questions about what things they didn't like, did like, what suggestions they had, what they wished they could have, what matters most to them, and so on.

When the responses came back, the internal product development department would tailor-make an offer to fit the need. They knew exactly what their audience wanted, and even more crucially, they also knew exactly who to contact with the new offer. The people who are ready to buy the offer, the hot buyers, are those people who responded to the surveys. Based on funnel attrition rates, his company could predict month-on-month sales.

Imagine you have a list of 100,000 people you can survey in your submarket. The first email you send out, inviting them to complete your survey, goes out to the entire 100,000. How many of those will actually open up the email?

According to Mailchimp, one of the largest email service providers in the world, it's about 20% to 25%, depending on your industry[1].

1   Email Marketing Benchmarks, Mailchimp, February 2017: https://mailchimp.com/resources/research/email-marketing-benchmarks/

Not everyone who opens your emails reads and clicks through to your survey page. In fact, the average clickthrough is about 20%.

So, if you started with 100,000 people, that would mean 20,000 people opened the email. Of that 20,000 (at 20% clickthrough), that would mean 4,000 people reached the survey page. Let's say only 20% of those actually completed the survey. That would give you 800 responses. That's less than 1%. In fact, it's a 0.008 (0.8%) response rate, and that's the industry standard with emails.

It differs from platform to platform. For example, a loyal and engaged social media fan base would have a higher percentage clickthrough rate. Also, as you probably realize, the larger the list, the more attrition. However, you will still have more conversions because of the larger number.

But we're not done yet!

That was just the first email to the list of 100,000. Let's say over the next 3 emails, we receive the same results, sticking with the 20% clickthrough rate. That would be 3,200 respondents, and these are your hot buyers!

Let's go a step further and assume 20% of those respondents bought the offer you created. You would have 640 buyers! Think about that for a minute. If you priced your offer at $150, you could predict sales of $96,000. What if your offer was priced at $1,500? Or more?

Matt's firm could make predictions like this and have a really good idea of what their profits could be before they created anything.

This strategy was so simple. It's like it should have been common knowledge all along.

For me to do this, I followed 4 steps:

1. Choose a market I like.
2. Find the audience group.
3. Find out what they want.
4. Package a solution and sell it to them.

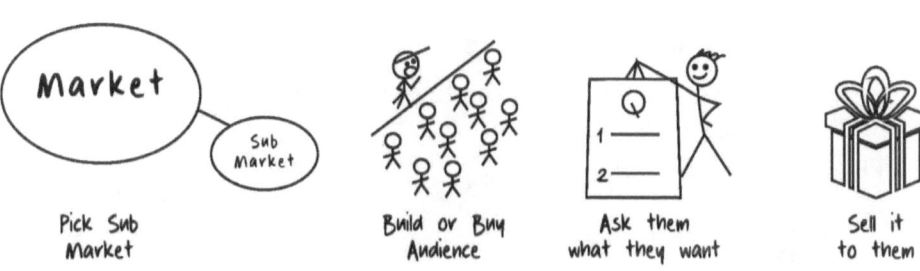

Pick Sub Market   Build or Buy Audience   Ask them what they want   Sell it to them

This 4-step process is a simple recipe for how to create your own niche offer. Once you know what people in your market want, all you need to do is find or create products or services as a solution. Pretty simple in the end, right?

This easy-to-understand concept should have been common knowledge to me since it's one of the first things you learn in most entry-level business marketing classes. They call this process primary research or field research, where statistical analyses glean qualitative and quantitative data from probability or non-probability samples. Yes, not very exciting, which is exactly why I completely forgot about the concept.

We tend to overcomplicate things (at least I can own up to it). But for concepts like this to stick, it's about how we are introduced to them and where we are in our life cycle. They have to become important enough to remember and act upon.

A dull teacher in an equally dull south London school classroom introduced this concept to me when I was around 15. So, it was not the opportune moment. At that time, the information had no other value to me except memorizing it for a short period to pass an exam.

However, these four steps were now the clear path forward I was looking for. I could step out of the fog and discover my niche offer.

The next day I started.

Step 1: Pick a Market, Not a Niche

I find that the easiest way to choose a market is through the process of elimination. We need to focus on excluding markets rather than including them.

I needed to be realistic. If I were going to wind down all my other ventures in favor of One Thing, it would need to be the Right Thing.

To do that, I needed to select a market I thought was the best fit for me and then go one level deeper into the submarket I wanted to be involved with. This is really important because when building or buying an audience, I would rather go narrow instead of wide. I'd much prefer an audience with 10,000 focused people or active buyers rather than 100,000 passively interested.

Each market you think of will have an infinite number of submarkets. Consider the fitness market, which is very broad, and you could be targeting anyone from people who play basketball to bodybuilding all the way through to yoga.

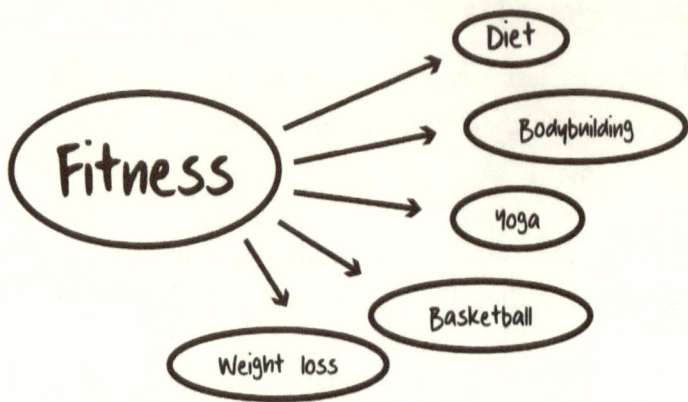

It's your job to choose a submarket. But remember not to make the mistake of picking someone else's niche. This means sticking with the submarket, not niches.

For example, with yoga, niches could be hot yoga, power yoga, or cardio yoga. With dieting, a niche could be high-fat, high-protein, low-carb, low-calorie, fasting diets through to muscle-building and sports-specific diets. We are not looking at those niches. This exercise is to help you carve out your own niche offer.

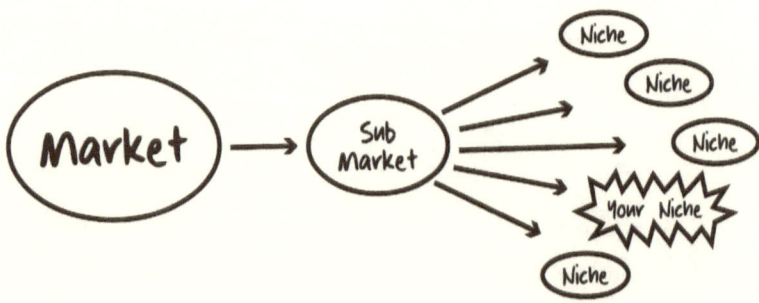

Sticking with the submarket is the key to your success. Your niche will be unique to you and separate you from the rest of the market.

In my case, I chose the business I was making the most money from. That submarket was alternative investments under the wealth market.

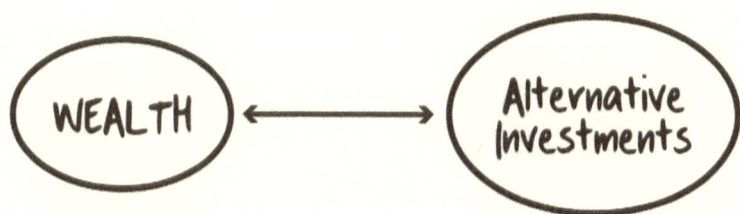

I was already involved with selling other people's niches within this submarket. At that time, I was selling real estate investments in student accommodation, senior and assisted-living properties, and other commercial and residential real estate, like hotels and multi-family and single-family properties. I was even involved with other alternative investment niches like selling precious gems, rare earth metals, fine art, and vintage wine bottles. These were ALL niches in the alternative investment submarket (AIM Market).

To create my own niche, I needed to compile a list or find a way to contact as many of the buyers within these niches. I call these groups of buyers Audience Groups. Once I do that, I can create a survey asking the right questions to figure out what unique offer I can create or find for them.

Action Plan

Choosing a Market and Submarket

- **Use process of elimination**: Focus on excluding markets to narrow down your options.

- **Be realistic and strategic**: Select a *market* that is the best fit for your goals and interests.

- **Go one level deeper into the submarket**: Choose a more focused submarket for a targeted audience. But remember, avoid the mistake of picking someone else's niche.

- **Understand the difference between submarkets and niches**: Recognize that each market has many submarkets, which are broader than niches.

In the next section, you will learn how to carve out your unique niche within the submarket you chose.

Step 2: Find Audience Groups

This is the point when we start looking for the audience within these niche buyer groups. The simplest and most effective way to do that is to look for WHO has already gathered these focused groups of people.

My goal is to locate the persons, places, or things that have the attention of buyers within a specific niche market. Once I identify those persons, places, and things, I can look to tap into their audiences. Then I could either build my own list by trying to draw members of these audience groups to my brand. Or better still, since I don't really have a brand yet and because this is still the research phase, we want to be as frugal as possible – and frugal is just a fancy word for being tight with your money.

These groups of people, my target audience, were looking for solutions within their chosen submarket and engaging in conversations, consuming content, and buying products and services within niches in that submarket. The easiest low-hanging fruit tended to be finding social media influencers, bloggers, podcasters, and other platforms and websites catering to those specific niche markets.

For example, if fitness is your market and yoga is the submarket, the audience groups I'm referring to are the people participating in niches like power yoga or hot yoga. Examples of your persons, places, and things could be the podcasts and social media influencers your audience group follows *(Persons)*. You have the forums, messenger groups, and websites they frequent and engage with *(Places)*. Then you have the products, specialized equipment, apps, software, and games they purchase and use *(Things)*. These Persons, Places, and Things have already gathered your audience groups with the added bonus that they also have the influence to sway the decisions and actively engage them!

Start by thinking about all these Persons, Places, and Things that could attract and hold the attention of your target audience groups.

Ask yourself:

- Which social media personalities do they follow?
- Which niche blogs or social media micro-blogs (X, Instagram) do they read?
- Which niche podcasts do they listen to?
- Which YouTube channels or shows do they watch?
- Which products or services do they purchase?
- Which conferences and events (online and offline) do they attend?
- Which books or magazines do they read?
- What type of websites do they go to?
- Which newsletters are they subscribed to?
- Which games do they play?
- Which apps or software do they use?
- What search terms do they Google?

To find results quickly and with very little effort, start with simple queries with an AI LLM (large language model) like ChatGPT and your bread-and-butter Google searches. You can create a simple prompt asking the LLM *"Create a list of what persons, places, and things that would hold the attention of my target audience in [Submarket]. Examples of this could include social media personalities, blogs, newsletters, books, podcasts, YouTube channels, events, apps, products, services, search terms, websites, etc. Please create a list of categories and specific names."*

You can play around with the prompts and responses to expand on the results, too. There's a degree of trial and error to expect here, but you'll quickly start to see a viable list, although it won't be exhaustive. However with the list you do get, you could then go to Google and expand it even further. Simply type in the name of your chosen submarket and one of the categories from the AI-generated list.

In the future, LLMs will probably be able to create a robust list for you. It's going to be awesome when that happens. But for now, this is the next logical step. So go ahead and create your list of categories and then go to Google and type in the name of your chosen submarket and then one of these categories.

E.g. [Submarket] + [category]

🔍 Yoga + Influencers

Blogs
Podcasts
YouTube
Books
and so on........

When I started searching, I found lots of social media personalities, from micro-influencers to mid-tier to thought leaders and social media celebrities with millions of followers. They could drive tens of thousands of people to pay attention to them and engage them.

I found blogs, both long format and micro ones, on social media platforms with thousands upon thousands of subscribers. Then I found podcasters who had listeners sitting through 2-hour podcast sessions. I found lots of companies with lists of customers, clients, newsletters, and warm prospects that were filled with audiences I wanted to talk to.

DistroList

As you conduct these searches and find results, start organizing them as a list with each category as the header.

Influencers	Blogs	Products	Video	Companies	Books
1.	1.	1.	1.	1.	1.
2.	2.	2.	2.	2.	2.
3.	3.	3.	3.	3.	3.
4.	4.	4.	4.	4.	4.

I call this my DistroList, and I will refer to this list throughout the rest of the book. It's the foundation for all the strategies and concepts I will explain later. So, it's really, REALLY important to do! In effect, this DistroList represents your universe of distribution channels that have the influence and authority to put your message in front of their cultivated and nurtured audience groups.

I recommend looking for 100+ results for each category so that you have enough to work with. You'll probably start finding it difficult to discover relevant results for each category after the first 20 or so. But keep digging deep to find those with the most focused, active, hyper-engaged, niche audience groups. The plan, after all, is to ask people if we can survey their audience. Most of them are going to tell you to stick that survey where the sun doesn't shine, but don't worry because I have a plan for that.

Once I complete my ChatGPT and Google searches to build my lists, I dig deeper using other online tools. I'll usually, in no particular order, go to Semrush, BuzzSumo, and Similarweb. These are some popular platforms at the time of this writing.

With Semrush, you can input a name/site of one of the persons, places, or things you put in your DistroList. The platform then tells you the biggest competitors for that site address based on the number of keywords. For example, if you put in poweryoga.com, Semrush would show you lots of other sites that compete for the same keywords as poweryoga.com. You'll find sites representing all sorts of persons, places, and things that never came up in your own initial searches.

With BuzzSumo, when you input a keyword like yoga, it returns a list of top content related to that keyword and the links to the websites where the content was found. These results could show things that were less obvious through to which social sites are ranking highest. For example, perhaps Instagram is buzzing with more yoga-related content than X (formerly Twitter), leading you to search for more there.

Similarweb, much like Semrush, will let you look at competitors who compete for the same keywords online but will also let you see the sites that refer the most traffic to a site and where that traffic goes after they leave the site. Yes, you can literally see where an audience is going after they leave that site, which can identify niches within your market you could have never imagined.

I know this is a manual process and can seem time-consuming, but trust me when I say that this is one of the best time, effort, and money investments you could make right now. I've followed this process for almost two decades under my company Core Agents. And now with DistroChannels, I've now been able to streamline the process using software and have built the DistroList app, which has search capability and built-in AI integrations to help make this super easy for you. You can try it for free at DistroList.app.

Action Plan

Finding Audience Groups

- **Identify who has gathered your target audience**: Look for influencers, bloggers, podcasters, and platforms that have already gathered people interested in your specific submarket.

- **Conduct targeted research**: Focus on finding where your target audience engages in conversations, consumes content, and makes purchases within your submarket.

- **List out Persons, Places, and Things**: Identify the key influencers (Persons), online communities and websites (Places), and products or services (Things) that your target audience interacts with.

Research and List Building

- **Ask yourself key questions**: Figure out what social media personalities, blogs, podcasts, products, events, and other resources your target audience follows or uses.

- **Use AI tools and Google searches**: Start with basic queries using AI tools like ChatGPT to create a list of categories relevant to your audience, and then refine and expand this list with Google searches.

- **Create a comprehensive DistroList**: Organize your findings into a list with each category as a header, aiming for 100+ results per category.

- **Dig deeper with online tools**: Use tools like Semrush, BuzzSumo, and Similarweb for further research. Input names or sites from your DistroList to find competitors and related content.

Building and Using Your DistroList

- **Expand and refine your list**: Continue to add to your DistroList, focusing on finding highly focused and active niche audience groups.

- **Leverage the DistroList App**: Use DistroList.app, which offers search capabilities and AI integrations, to streamline the process.

Additional Steps

- **Persistence in research**: Acknowledge that the process is manual and time-consuming but essential for finding the right audience groups.

- **Use advanced online tools**: Explore further with advanced features of online tools to uncover less obvious connections and traffic patterns related to your submarket.

▨ Step 3: Ask Them What They Want

Back in 2009, I remember watching an episode of the *Dragons' Den*, UK's equivalent of *Shark Tank*, and one of the Dragons, James Caan, offered advice to one of the contestants. He said something along the lines of, "The answer you're looking for is usually in someone else's head. It's simply your job to find the people with the answers you're looking for and ask the right questions. Most of the time, they'll tell you what you want to know. You'd be surprised how willing people are to help if you simply ask." I remembered this especially because around the same time I heard someone else saying something similar, "If you don't ask, you don't get." Once you realize this remarkably convenient truth, it makes getting the answers you want less daunting and super simple.

Since you know who your audience groups are and which person, place, or thing has their attention, you've already done the first part. You found the people who have the answers you want, and you know where they are. Now all you have to do is ask those groups of people what they want.

This is usually the point where most people get a little stuck. Initially, it sounds simple and straightforward, but those who try it will quickly realize that knowing what to ask, where to ask it, and how to actually ask it can be a bit tricky.

You essentially have 3 little jobs:

1. **What to ask:** Which question(s) will you ask that will
   a. Give you enough responses and
   b. Be useful?

2. **Where to ask**: Where will the question be asked so that:
   a. It's easy for the audience groups to complete and
   b. It's also easy for you to analyze the responses when the survey is over?
3. **How to ask**: What strategy will you use to get the audience groups to complete the survey? Will you
   a. Collaborate with the persons, places, or things in your DistroList and ask them to ask their audience for you (best) or
   b. Pay to send ads targeting their audience groups with links to your survey (second best)?

I'm going to share the simplest, cheapest, and fastest way to do this, in my opinion. There are many ways to probe and survey audience groups to get qualitative and quantitative data, which big businesses spend a lot of resources on. But if you're reading this book, you're looking for a proven strategy that cuts through the noise, like how a hot knife cuts through butter. And that the strategy is preferably low cost or no cost, easy to do, and when done correctly, will lead to lots of profit… am I right?

Okay good, then I have just the thing for you.

What to Ask

Bearing in mind that these audience groups are NOT your existing clients, you don't want to bombard them with too many questions. In fact, what we really want is ONE question that is clever enough to give us lots of responses where we can easily identify and measure the intensity of similar answer clusters and rank the responses. You might think this will be a super-scientific query, but it can actually be pretty simple and easy for your audience groups to answer. (The suspense is killing me… drumroll…)

Simply ask them this:

If you could ask just ONE question about _____, what would it be?

Simple, right? When people answer this question, you can quickly see what these audience groups care about most. Granted, some people may provide answers they think are correct, what they think is a smart response, or what they think you want to hear. But if you have a large enough audience, you will receive lots of responses where you can quickly identify answer clusters in which responses are closely related.

And before you bite my head off, yes, there are other questions you can ask. Here are some other alternatives or additional questions you could use that are super slick in getting the information you want without you or the person asking them sounding like one of those boring surveys:

- What's the trickiest part about [Submarket] that keeps you up at night?

- Picture your dream scenario in [Submarket]. What would it look like?

- Where do you turn to get your information about [Submarket]? Any favorite books, blogs, or podcasts?

- How do you handle [Submarket] challenges like a pro?

- If you had to choose one aspect of [Submarket] to focus on right now, what would it be?

- What would take your [Submarket] experience from good to amazing?

- What specific qualities make a [Submarket] product or service irresistible to you?

- What factors sway your decision when it's time to make a purchase in [Submarket]?

- How do you prefer to soak up information about [Submarket]? Are you all about videos, articles, or live events?

- If you could wave a magic wand, what additional support or resources would make your [Submarket] experience extraordinary?

Whichever one you use will help you quickly identify and group responses where your audience is asking for the same thing in different ways. This will drown out the untrue or misleading responses. Therefore, the largest answer cluster would reflect your most common questions about your submarket. This information will tell you what you need to put together to carve out your niche in the market.

Where to Ask

Now that we have your question(s), we need to put it (them) in a place that's easily accessible and where it can pool all the responses.

Many social platforms provide audience engagement tools that offer these survey options, but doing it that way limits your surveys reach because your responses and analytics are coming in from one platform at a time. This can get quite messy.

My go-to options are the tools that let you create your own landing page that you provide links to. This allows you or anyone else to post that link on any platform. It can be placed on Facebook, Instagram, TikTok, Threads, X, YouTube, email, or even in display/banner ads. All the clickthroughs on any of those platforms go to one place where the results are pooled and only accessible by you.

My favorite go-to options are:

- SurveyMonkey
- ClickFunnels
- Mailchimp
- Constant Contact

These software options, which are easy to use, allow you to create a simple online mini-survey in the form of a simple landing page. I have used all these, and they are great dummy-proof solutions for getting a professional page that can automatically adjust for desktop and mobile views. Plus, they each have nice back-office dashboards where you can see all the responses and analytics.

It's important to capture the names and emails of the people taking the survey. In addition to the names and emails, I also invite them to provide their mobile/cell numbers or join a messenger group so that I can notify them of the results when the survey ends.

This data capture step is crucial because the people who answer this survey will be your low-hanging fruit. You are literally creating a tailor-made offer for them at a time when they want it. Your job is to get an offer in front of them as soon as possible.

How to Ask

The next mini-job is to get that survey out in front of the right audience groups. Since we know who already holds their attention and that they should be nicely organized in your DistroList, this should be pretty straightforward.

You literally have 3 options:

1. Collaborate with the people in your DistroList and have them ask their audiences for you for free,
2. Pay for the collaboration with a fee for them to distribute your questionnaire as part of an industry research exercise, or
3. Send ads directly to their audiences using platforms like Google and Facebook.

Unpaid Collaboration

I extensively cover many of these collaboration strategies and audience engagement techniques later in this book. But for now, I will share with you my very own standard practice, which always gets me results.

It's a simple script you will use to either prepare an email, a direct message (DM) on social media platforms, or when you pick up the phone and call the person or business directly.

Hey [Prospect's Name],

I hope you're doing great! I came across your [Profile/Product/Business], and it got me really excited about the research I'm conducting on [Submarket]. I think your audience demographics align perfectly with my project.

I've already teamed up with some amazing partners like [Business/Influencer 1], [Business/Influencer 2], and [Business/Influencer 3]. I'd love to have you onboard, too!

By joining our collaboration, you'll have exclusive access to collaboration options and all the analytics we uncover. Trust me, it's going to be a game-changer for understanding your audience.

I'd like to chat with you further about this. How about tomorrow at [Time]? But, if that doesn't work for you, just let me know, and we'll find a time that suits us both.

Thanks for considering this. I'm really looking forward to the potential of working together. Feel free to shoot me any questions or if you need more info.

Take care,
[Your Name]

You don't need to copy this example exactly, so feel free to personalize it as you see fit. However, there are a few essentials I'd recommend you keep in there that prepare your prospect (and you) for the final step.

These are as follows:

- Name-drop competitors from your DistroList. The closer the competitors are to their niche, the better. This goes for influencers, too.

- Emphasize that you are researching their submarket, not their niche. You want them to feel like they are being invited to participate in a larger market.

- Let them know you checked out their profile/product/ business so that they know this was not a spam message.

- Share what's in it for them by letting them know how future collaborations could work along with giving them all the analytics, which they can leverage immediately.

- Embed a strong call to action with a date/time to talk further.

Let me share some insights on what you should expect throughout this outreach exercise. I had you create a DistroList with 100+ names in each category because 80% of them will say NO or simply ignore your request when you do reach out like this.

But the 20% who do will give you the keys to the castle. And many of those who said NO initially or who flat-out ignored you will be lining up to work with you later on down the road. All you need to do is stick to the plan.

Paid Research Collaboration

If people in your distribution list won't collaborate for free, even after you've name-dropped the other individuals or potential partnerships you're working with, the issue might be in your approach or the people you're approaching. Perhaps they are full of self-importance or even a bit snobby. I don't know, but that's why we have options.

In this situation, consider offering payment for participating in a research survey, with the promise of sharing the results with them. This approach may seem unconventional, but it's actually quite slick. You can offer to pay them a fee to distribute your questionnaire as part of an industry research exercise. This works especially well with influencers, podcasters, and other business types who revolve around publishing as a core activity.

Your pitch remains essentially the same. You are collaborating with several companies or individuals in your field. You are offering a fee for distributing your questionnaire. And, you will also be offering to share the results from all your surveys. Honestly, you could even charge an additional fee for providing the final combined report. I've seen it done plenty of times.

However, I want you to recognize that If you do charge them for the report, you risk a higher upfront fee that you need to pay them. I have always offered to supply the combined report for free so that

I can negotiate a smaller fee or even move the collaboration back to free if I can. I'll leave that decision to you.

When asked about your motivation for doing this, simply explain that your goal is to better serve the market and that you are considering the possibility of developing a joint product offering in the future. This response is sufficiently vague, but it directly addresses their question while also subtly laying the groundwork for your upcoming offer, which I will discuss more in the 'Your Offer' section of this part.

Imagine approaching 3 different yoga businesses, 3 car dealerships, or 3 dentists. You tell them you're offering an incentivized market research campaign where you will pay them to survey their own audience and that you are working with other businesses in the same market. And as a reward for their participation, you will also give them access to the final report with *ALL* the results combined.

Do you think you could convince people to find out more about their customers and what they want, with you footing the bill? Sounds like a no-brainer!

When I was setting up my financial marketing business for selling alternative investments, I used this strategy A LOT. I remember creating a quick website on Wix.com for my consulting and market research company and having a team member contact our competitors and offer them this type of paid survey. It worked extremely well at gaining access to the clients I wanted and finding out exactly what they were looking for. I then collaborated with my so-called competitors to actually create the thing the market wanted. More on this later in the offer creation section.

To get you started, here's a simple script you could send to influencers:

Hi [Influencer's Name],

We'll pay you to share our survey!

I'm [Your Name] from [Your Company]. We like what you're doing in [Profile/Product/Business] and believe it aligns with our research in the [Submarket] sector.

We'd like to pay you to promote an industry survey for us. It's not just about the payment. You'll also get exclusive insights from the final survey results from all the other people and businesses we are working with so that you can understand what your audience wants.

Interested in this paid collaboration? Let's discuss the details – are you free to chat tomorrow at [Time]? If not, let me know what works for you.

Looking forward to the possibility of working together!

Best,
[Your Name]

For businesses you are approaching, you could write something more formal like this:

Subject: Opportunity for Paid Participation in Industry Research – Access Comprehensive Insights

Hi [Prospect's Name],

I hope this message finds you well. I'm [Your Name] from [Your Company].

I'd like to extend an invitation for you to participate in a paid survey. We think your [Product/Business] aligns with our current research initiative in the [Submarket] sector. This isn't just about the monetary reward, though. You'll also gain exclusive access to a detailed report encompassing the collective results from the people and businesses we are working with so that you can understand what your customers (and your competitors' customers!) want.

This data could provide valuable insights for your business strategy.

We're collaborating with industry leaders like [Business/ Influencer 1 from your DistroList], [Business/Influencer 2 from your DistroList], and [Business/Influencer 3 from your DistroList], and your participation would add significant value. We assure complete confidentiality of your responses.

I'd love to discuss this further with you. Are you available for a chat tomorrow at [Time]? If that doesn't work, please suggest a time that does.

Thank you for considering this opportunity. Please don't hesitate to contact me for further details.

Best regards,
[Your Name]

For everyone in your DistroList agreeing to work with you, **whether it's the unpaid collaboration or through the paid research campaign,** simply give them a link to the online survey page you created. They can then share that link with their audience through whatever platform they wish. You could even guide them on what to say to their audience if you think it will help.

> *Hey [Prospect's Name],*
>
> *Hope you're doing well! We're reaching out to gather insights about what really matters to you in [Submarket].*
>
> *If you had the chance to ask us a single question about [Submarket], what would it be? We'd love to hear your thoughts and value your input.*
>
> *Just a quick click on the following [Link] will take you to a short form where you can share your question with us. It won't take much of your time, and we genuinely appreciate your participation.*
>
> *Thanks a million for being a part of this!*
>
> *Warm regards,*
> *[Your Name]*

In a perfect world, everyone in your DistroList will say YES and promote your survey to their audience. If that were the case, you'd never need to worry about spending money on advertising. Unfortunately, the world does not work that way.

About 80% of the people in your DistroList (or more) will not promote your market research survey for you, and we haven't even reached the selling part yet! However, that thankfully is not the only way to get in front of their audience. If they do not want to work with you, then like the age-old saying, "money talks," this is your opportunity to let a little money do the talking for you.

Ads

You can also run paid ads to their audience directly, using the available marketing features on platforms like Google and Facebook. Pretty much all social media platforms give advertisers (you) a way to send ads to the fans of influential people or specific social media accounts. Granted, sending ads this way is less powerful than an endorsed promotion. You don't benefit from having the authority in their sphere of influence personally requesting their loyal and faithful audience to fill in your survey.

But sending ads is the next best thing. Plus, even if some people in your DistroList said they wanted nothing to do with you or your business, which happened to me plenty of times, there's literally nothing they can do to stop you from targeting their audiences anyway! That's why it is so important for you to create your DistroList.

If you are going to create an ad, there are a few guidelines to follow to be effective. Just because you've identified where your audience groups are and how to get a message in front of them, your job is not done. You still need to get their attention so that they actually "see" the ad, click it, and hopefully take the survey.

Designing an ad, or at least knowing what makes an ad good, is essential knowledge for someone starting out in business. Ad creation is by far one of the most important skills to develop, regardless of what you sell or who you sell it to. Its purpose is simple – to get people to stop what they are doing and start reading or watching whatever it is you put in front of them.

But here's the deal – there's already a ton of information out there dedicated to sales collateral and marketing funnels, and it's a deep ocean to swim in. But don't worry because I've got your back! Instead of diving deep into all that stuff right now, I'll give you the essentials you need to create your survey ad right now. Let's keep it simple and get you on track!

To begin, we need a catchy headline. If the headline sucks, no one will click on your ad, watch your videos, read your blog, or take your survey. You want to create something that grabs people's attention, stops them in their tracks, and makes them pay attention. To do that, we'll use one of the oldest (probably ancient) sales and marketing tactics that accomplishes this, without fail, every time. And that is to successfully interrupt someone and turn that **interruption into an interaction**. To do this, simply ask them a question.

It's an age-old strategy that's been hammered into my mind in any sales and marketing environment I've ever been in. Simple, right? Here's the better news. You already have a powerful question that will serve as your headline for this ad. Some of you may be familiar with ads and recognize that what I'm talking about is a pattern interrupt attention grabber. If you have some experience in this space and have other headliner ideas, please feel free to personalize them as you see fit. However, this headliner is designed purposefully for this sequence, so please stick with me.

Your headline:

If you could ask just ONE question about _____, what would it be?

Now, all you need to do is pair this headline up with an image or video that drives curiosity like the headline does.

Pro Tip

Make no mistake… when you're marketing to someone, you are interrupting whatever they are doing. However, you can turn this interruption into something valuable, so think of your outreach as a friendly conversation. By creating questions that resonate and engage, you're turning a simple interruption into an opportunity to meaningfully connect with your audience on what matters most to them. This shift from interruption to interaction helps build genuine relationships and ensures that your outreach is customer-focused and impactful. Remember, a well-crafted question can be the bridge that turns strangers into interested participants.

For this type of one-question survey, I find that using a meme is a great way to grab someone's attention long enough to ask them a question. Memes come in many forms. They can be funny, thought-provoking, aspirational, relatable, interactive, nostalgic, controversial (with caution), behind the scenes memes, and even educational. Just make sure the meme itself is actually relevant to your submarket and your ask. Since this is an interactive ad, the idea is to design a meme that encourages audience participation.

Let me break down some of your options:

Funny Meme: Create a meme with humor related to your survey topic.

Thought-Provoking Meme: Create a meme that poses a question or presents a thought-provoking scenario.

Interesting Meme: Share an interesting fact or statistic related to your survey in a visually appealing way.

Aspirational Meme: Inspire your audience with a meme conveying positive and aspirational messaging.

Relatable Meme: Create a meme that taps into shared experiences or common situations that are universally recognizable and connect it to your survey topic.

Nostalgic Meme: Appeal to nostalgia by incorporating elements from the past that resonate with your audience, such as popular culture from the past.

Controversial Meme (with caution): Address a controversial or debated topic within your niche to spark discussions, such as a bold opinion or statement related to your survey topic. Just be mindful that controversy could lead to potential backlash.

Behind-the-Scenes Meme: Offer a glimpse behind the scenes of your project, business, or survey creation process with candid or funny examples.

Educational Meme: Combine concise information with visuals to educate your audience on a relevant subject in a visually appealing and easy-to-understand way.

You're probably wondering which one to start with? The simple answer is to start with the one you like most and rotate through them all until you find the one that works best for your audience. Maybe you'll have ads running with each one of them!

If we stick to our fitness market with yoga being the submarket, I would want a catchy yoga meme to pair with my headline. You could easily go to Google or Pinterest and search "[Submarket] memes" or "funny [Submarket] memes." Doing this will give you a lot of options to choose from or use as examples for creating your own.

A quick word of caution with copyright laws and fair use guidelines. Since memes have become a significant part of internet culture, some people have even turned them into a business through licenses and advertising. Because of that, some meme creators will get upset if you use their pictures without permission, and they can take legal action. We don't want that. It's essential not to mess with someone's ability to make money from their own work.

Fair use guidelines exist, in part, to allow people to create and share original works, and there are a few factors that determine whether you're safe to engage with a popular meme. I'll spare you the full legal context and cut to the chase. Creating and sharing original memes, even using copyrighted material in a transformative way, is generally acceptable under fair use. Translated, this means that you can use memes for things like surveys without any problems. But using them to make money or fundraising might lead to legal issues. So for you, and as my disclaimer, that means using a meme for a survey ad is good, but for a buy-it-now ad is bad. Are we clear on that?

Okay, so once you find or create your image, pair it with your headline question and use the recommended text we offered people in your DistroList earlier.

Pro Tip

Memes are a fantastic and quick way to engage your audience, but you can apply the same strategy to any hot and trending content! Explore topics that are buzzing on social media by using social listening apps like Buzzsumo, Hootsuite, Sprout Social, and Mention to name a few. I mentioned some larger brands there since they are likely to stick around longer, but there are new companies popping up every day that specialize in finding trending content. All of these apps will help you keep an ear to the ground, identifying what people are talking about, and most of them have a free trial, too. Once you spot a trending topic, get creative and repurpose it in a way that connects with your audience. Whether it's a popular hashtag, viral challenge, or trending theme, adapting and incorporating these trends into your content can help you stay relevant and capture attention. So, keep an eye on what's hot, and turn those trends into content that turns your interruption into an interaction!

Your ad would look something like this:

When people click that ad, they will be taken to the landing page you created. Your ad is the question, and the question is your survey. It's relevant to your submarket, and as I said before, you'll be surprised at how many people will respond by simply having been asked the question! Once that's done, move to the next step.

Action Plan

What to Ask

- **Create a simple and clever question**: Create a question that elicits meaningful responses, such as "If you could ask just ONE question about [Submarket], what would it be?"
- **Consider alternative questions**: Use other questions to get diverse insights like challenges in the submarket or dream scenarios.

Where to Ask

- **Choose a suitable platform for surveys**: Opt for platforms that allow easy creation and distribution of surveys, such as SurveyMonkey, ClickFunnels, Mailchimp, or Constant Contact.
- **Create a landing page for the survey**: Ensure it's easy to complete and analyze.

How to Ask

- **Decide on the approach for distribution**: Collaborate with those in your DistroList to distribute the survey or pay to send ads targeting your audience.

Unpaid Collaboration

- **Use a personalized script for outreach**: Approach people on your DistroList with a personalized message, expressing interest in collaborating in the survey.
- **Emphasize mutual benefits**: Highlight the advantages of the collaboration, such as access to combined analytics.

Paid Research Collaboration

- **Consider paying for participation**: If unpaid collaboration isn't possible, offer payment for distributing your questionnaire.
- **Explain the benefits**: Emphasize access to the final combined survey results and the potential for future joint products.

Ads for Survey Promotion

- **Use ads for a broader reach**: If collaboration fails, resort to paid ads on platforms like Google and Facebook, targeting specific audiences.
- **Create engaging ad content**: Design an ad with an attention-grabbing headline and an accompanying image or video.
- **Ensure the ad leads to your survey**: The ad should directly link to your survey landing page.

Using Memes in Ads

- **Select an appropriate meme**: Choose a meme that resonates with your audience and relates to your survey topic.
- **Be mindful of copyright laws**: Use or create original memes within fair use guidelines.
- **Pair the meme with your survey question**: Use the meme to engage your audience and encourage them to participate in the survey.

Staying Relevant With Trending Content

- **Monitor social media trends**: Use social listening apps like BuzzSumo or Hootsuite to identify trending topics.

- **Incorporate trends into your content**: Adapt trending themes into your survey promotion strategy to increase engagement.

Advanced Difficulty

- Once you have the basics, over time you can **fine-tune your survey questions** to provide more comprehensive insights.

- Experiment with A/B testing to **optimize your survey landing page** and ad performance.

Step 4: Sell It to Them

The results from your survey should clearly indicate what your submarket cares about most, even if you have an abysmal turnout and only a handful of people in your DistroList agreed to send it out to their audiences. Perhaps you paid them a fee or sent out a targeted ad on a small budget. If you've done either one or a combination of these, your DistroList should bring in lots of valuable responses that you can draw conclusions from. So, what are you going to sell them?

At this stage, you should have a good understanding of what your submarket really wants based on the questions they asked you. You should be thinking up lots of ideas and solutions. But you'll probably have some fears, worries, and doubts crop up, too. This is to be expected.

Some of the questions floating through your mind may sound like the following:

- Where will I get the money to create this?
- Do I have the right solution based on what they are asking?
- What if I make a mistake?
- Are they really going to buy this?
- Is my solution a good idea, or will it be a fad and fizzle out?
- How will the people in my DistroList respond?
- Do I develop my own offer, or do I sell under someone else's brand?

These, and any other thoughts you may have, are all valid! Your audience told you what they want, but it still leaves you open to a lot of variables and risks. As you go through this process, you'll soon find yourself facing 3 doors.

Door #1: Create and develop your own offering that you fully fund and take to market.

Door #2: Sell another company or brand's products and services as a solution.

Door #3: Come up with a blend of both.

This is a good place to be! Remind yourself that you have a list of hot buyers, where a large percentage are likely to buy your offer. Of course, the solution you've come up with must be sensible. It should be priced well and do whatever it promises, meaning it needs to work.

Additionally, you're probably thinking about whether this will stand the test of time. Without me analyzing the results you have, there's no way for me to tell you whether your idea has the potential to scale up or if it's a short-term fad that's only filling a short-term need. But also, I'm no expert in that market, and at this point, neither are you. So, deciding whether it's better to create your own product or sell another company's products is a question with pros and cons.

For starters, many products and services are available for you to choose from. They are already built, they've been tested, and they're clearly selling. In fact, you may choose to work with a brand with a lot of recognition, which is easy to promote. Working with someone else's brand means it's ready to sell immediately so that you can capitalize on your hot prospects straight away.

On the flip side, if the product or service does not sell so well, you can easily switch to something different. You could even promote multiple brands, helping you spread your risk and benefit from more overall sales. That's no guarantee, but it worked out well for Amazon. Remember, they started as an online bookstore.

Then there's the other side. Since you are essentially a middleman, you can easily be circumvented because it's generally difficult to get exclusive agreements, even if you are well-established.

Also, your profit margins may not be high enough with the product or service you like. That means you have to choose to sell lesser comparables, which does you and your customers a disservice. Plus, along with settling for lower-quality products, you may be dealing with lots of other people selling the same thing and bloodying the water with too much competition. This quickly forces you away from your niche audience and back into the wider market. You could find yourself trapped, selling sub-par offers that many other people are also selling to the same audience.

If you create your own product or service, you can focus on your niche and serve your own audience group as best as you can. But it is up to you to develop a viable business or product, which can be very time-consuming and costly. And let's be honest, you could screw it up even if it is a good idea, and you wouldn't be the first or last!

I'm not telling you all this to dishearten you. I've been down this road plenty of times, and I've actually come up with a solution that aligns with everything I've said so far. It works like a charm every time I do it! As I reveal it to you, you'll see how everything you've done so far has been a sequence leading up to this point. I call this the we-listened campaign, which I'm about to teach you.

Creating Your Offer

Before we start, let me remind you that this book is meant to be a recipe book that comes directly from my own experiences in setting up and growing businesses. It will help entrepreneurs, at any level, set up and grow their businesses.

Unlike typical theory-heavy textbooks or books written by supposed business gurus who *claim* to cover every possible strategy, this book shares what I've actually done and found success with. I won't cover every possible way to create an offer here. I want to focus on delivering what works and will make you succeed instead of throwing useless information at you. Is that a fair deal?

I've spent a ton of time working on my own businesses and helping others figure out their go-to-market strategies and what they're bringing to the table in terms of an offer. Not because I was doing it out of favor or for charity. I helped others build their businesses up because it helped me build my own business. I succeeded, and they succeeded. It was a win-win.

Through that experience, I've learned you don't need the best product out there to make your business a hit. But you do need to be smart about your strategic position so that when you do actually make the offer, people will want to buy it. Your potential customers told you what they want, so your job here is to create an offer that is good enough to meet their expectations and delivers on what it promises. For example, if your audience asks for anti-aging cream, don't repackage and sell them sunscreen.

Remember, the market has already done the hard work, so let's give it to them.

The We-Listened Campaign

So, what we're going to do is look to minimize our overall risk regarding product development expenses and with reducing the worry and anxiety of whether you're creating something that will actually be good.

This is by far the fastest route I have ever encountered to becoming a leader in your submarket. It's the fastest way I know to create your own unique niche offer and get it to market under your own brand.

The method I'm about to describe takes almost all the product development pressure off your shoulders while ensuring that your offer can deliver what it promises. This means you can make money while you rest easy, knowing that what you've sold is actually doing what it's supposed to do.

To begin, you must first go back to your results. We want to choose 3 questions. These questions could be either the Top 3 that came through your results or perhaps 3 others with enough of a response rate you feel need answering.

This is literally the definition of identifying a need and filling it. It's business basics 101, and it doesn't get more basic than this. Once you identify your Top 3 questions, we will flip those questions into Benefit Statements.

For example, if you sent that survey to audience groups in the yoga submarket, you may have received questions like:

- How do I accurately calculate calories burned in a yoga session?
- Is there an official yoga diet for weight loss?
- Can static yoga poses build muscle?

I made those up. In fact, those were the objections I made to my wife whenever she tried to talk me into taking up yoga. However, these will work to illustrate my point. Next, we need to turn those questions into benefit statements. To do that, we will follow a few easy formulas.

How to _____ so that you can _____.

You can _____ without _____.

It _____, which means _____.

How every _____ can _____.

There are many ways to do this, and you can mix and match these in a few different ways.

Here's what I did with my yoga example:

- **How to** track your calorie burn during a yoga session **so that you can** better evaluate your performance.
- **Learn the** optimal yoga diet **so that you can** drop weight **without** energy loss and still eat chocolate.
- **How** static yoga poses could help you build muscles, **which means** you can become stronger while maintaining flexibility and balance.

Just remember to describe the feature and then explain how it benefits the potential buyer. Simple enough, right? I want to show you how to cultivate and leverage relationships so that you can mass collaborate and enter ANY market, carve out your own niche, and build your own business that will immediately be known as a brand that delivers on its promises. Now let me show you how to create a unique, tangible offer.

#1: Collaboration

As you might have guessed, I suggest reaching out to people on your DistroList and collaborating with them to create a solution for each of those benefit statements. Or another way to put it is that you're going to work with those people to deliver on the promises you are about to make. Here's what I mean.

Once you have your Top 3 Benefit Statements, we're going to draft sales copy. And this is where the magic happens...

Hi _____, we listened!

So, we teamed up with [Business/Influencer 1 from your DistroList], [Business/Influencer 2 from your DistroList], and [Business/Influencer 3 from your DistroList] to show you how to:

- *[Benefit Statement 1]*
- *[Benefit Statement 2]*
- *[Benefit Statement 3]*

Check it out here!

If we look at my fictional yoga case study, it would go something like this:

Hi _____, we listened!

So, we teamed up with Bikram Yoga, CorePower Yoga, and Yogi Stats to show you how to:

- *Track your calorie burn during your yoga sessions so that you can better evaluate your performance.*
- *Learn the optimal yoga diet so that you can drop weight without energy loss or giving up chocolate!*
- *How static yoga poses could help you build lean muscle fast, which means you become stronger while maintaining flexibility and balance.*

Check it out here!

As you can see from that script, I'm suggesting you bring in the other people and businesses you collaborated with to create the offer. This isn't an absolute requirement, but it will help you go to market faster. It doesn't need to be three, you could simply partner with one if you want. But the goal is to have these solutions created under *your brand*. You are cutting them into a deal, not the other way around. It is you who found out what the audience in that submarket wants and who is about to take the steps to create a tailor-made solution(s) for them.

You are essentially collaborating with other people and businesses in your DistroList to build out exactly what your audience wants, at the exact time they want it. Just like how you tap into the influence they have with their audiences, you can also tap into the experience, expertise, connections, and infrastructure they have in creating products or services in that submarket, too. Collaborating this way means you are partnering up with other businesses to create the supply for the demand you will be generating.

If you remember, I spoke about this in Part 1: Empower Yourself, Earn Instantly, where I said you could collaborate with a company and have them build your own unique product. This entire section uses that as its founding principle. What I'm saying is that you can pick a specific company, or a selection of people and companies to work with, from your DistroList and create your own unique offer with them. Because you know what your audience wants, you could take something that is pre-existing and simply enhance the product, add any necessary features, or even repackage the offer to fit the bill.

This arrangement would secure exclusive distribution rights, making you the only seller of this improved product. And consequently, this increases the product's value and its price point, too! Exclusivity like this is powerful in setting yourself apart from the other players in the market. Its uniqueness and rarity alone can drive up demand, and since it's being sold under your brand, it means you have your own business with an offer you know you can deliver on.

The best part is the partner company is dealing with all the logistics, fulfillment, and customer service, and you can sleep soundly knowing they can deliver on what they promise because they have a solid track record. Doing it this way means you'll be taking a smaller slice of the pie, but the pie itself will be much larger and more sustainable.

I'll go into pricing in the next section, but I wanted to quickly mention it here as I'm sure you're already thinking about how big that slice is for you. My general rule of thumb when it comes to collaborations is that if you do the lion's share of the work, you should take 70% and carve out 30% for partners. If the partners you bring on take the task of building out the product or delivering the service, while you provide the hot buyers, then you take 30%, leaving 70% for them. For example, if a company creates a unique product for you, manages the logistics and fulfillment, and deals with all the customer service, while you focus solely on making money on the sales, they would take 70% and leave 30% for you. This type of arrangement is highly favorable to you from a risk-reward perspective, and it also incentivizes the company to provide you with a quality product and excellent support since their earnings are directly tied to the product's success in the market.

This can be applied to creating almost any type of offer. I've even done this in real estate investment deals. I remember collaborating with two real estate investment firms to repurpose existing property based on what the target audience wanted at the time. You may remember coworking office space being a big buzzword in the real estate world, but people also started looking into co-living spaces, too. We saw an opportunity to buy an apartment building in New York and turn it into a hip co-living space. I literally teamed up with two other real estate investment firms from our DistroList to pick a good location and work together under a new brand to deal with all the legal, operations, and refurbishment costs to build out the project.

Our teamwork paid off big time, too. People felt good about buying into the project because they trusted the other companies involved, and they liked the fact that those respected and established businesses in the real estate world were teaming up on this project.

In the end, I made 30% on the profits of the sale while the other two firms split the 70% profit between themselves. This collaboration made it much quicker to sell the investment opportunity, and it showed me how working together can create a really exciting and trusted offer in the market.

Even though I made less money on the deal, it was much less of an operational headache. My position of leverage was that I had the list of hot buyers ready to allocate money while those companies had the experience, connections, and resources to get the job done fast. Like the old saying goes, it's better to have 30% of something than 100% of nothing.

Having said all that, it's not essential for you to work with other companies to create the offer. That suggestion was simply that… a suggestion. I highlighted this technique because it helps with credibility. You will be leveraging theirs. But ultimately, the choice is yours. By all means, if you want to create your offer independently, do exactly that. You've done enough research with this framework to know exactly what your audience wants.

Let's go through some other options for building out your product or service quickly so that you can start making money fast!

#2: Private Label AKA White Label

This option is one of the easiest ways to start selling your own brand of products. You don't need to worry about going through the entire research and development process where you design, prototype, manufacture, and everything else in between.

All you need to do is find an existing product and brand it with your logo, color scheme, information, packaging, and so on. You can usually make small design changes with private label manufacturers at low-to-no upfront costs.

For physical products or merchandise, Alibaba is by far the most popular platform for sourcing private label products from China and other foreign countries. However, you can also white label software packages, too.

When I was in the recruitment business, I once had a sales and leadership aptitude test that was accessed through a portal on my website. When a candidate logged into the platform, they could choose from a multitude of tests that they could pay to take. The cool thing was I didn't spend a penny developing it. I simply paid an online testing software company to use their sophisticated and very well-built testing software under my company's brand. After an initial setup fee, I paid them a monthly fee based on the number of tests my candidates took.

Private labeling is especially useful when there is already a product that exists for another market, but it could also be used as a solution for your niche. A great example is how protective knee pads for skateboarders and cyclists could also be used to protect the knees of bricklayers on construction jobs.

This is usually referred to as a substitute product, which can act as a solution to a need, e.g., your niche. You make money quite quickly if you can find a substitute product, brand it in line with your niche, and offer it to your target audiences.

#3: Original Equipment Manufacturer (OEM)

This is where you intend to create an original product from the ground up. It's a much more involved process, and you'll be working closely with designers and manufacturers to go from the idea phase to prototyping, through to testing, and finally, a finished marketable product.

If you have an idea for a very unique product and not on the market already, this is the way to go. Equally, you may also consider this option if the design changes you want to make to a private-label product are more than the manufacturer is willing to make.

I faced this option when I was creating the Yummy Bar chocolate. I was essentially private-labeling my own brand of chocolate at first. I simply chose a flavor of chocolate pellets (dark chocolate, milk chocolate, mint, etc.), which would be melted down and poured into molds to be hardened into bars. I chose the shape of the bar from a selection the chocolate manufacturer already had. They allowed us to imprint our logo, Yummy Bar, on the chocolate bar, but that was about as far as they'd go for modifications. If I wanted to change the shape of the bar and go with something other than the traditional breakable cubed design, I needed to create my own molds. For example, I needed to consider my own OEM equipment to start creating layered chocolate with caramel or nougat variants.

You'll find yourself facing similar decision trees whether you are creating your own clothing brand, fitness equipment company, cooking and cutlery business… you name it. This applies to pretty much anything you want to create that's not already available. So, provided you did your research, which you have done if you followed the steps in this section, you know what your buyer groups want, and this could be a viable option.

#4 Digital Products

Do you want to create a medical app that combines wearable tech, social media, and the metaverse to create a deeply immersive, gamified experience to tackle PTSD? Well, if you wanted to, you can, albeit that sort of digital product might take a bit of time and a lot of money to get going.

Digital products can range from super simple to unbelievably complex. You can go from creating a digital membership, which might give you access to a few downloadable PDFs and how-to videos, or you could make more complex apps and SaaS products. You could even look to the bleeding edge of what's possible with the most futuristic technology and create a solution for your niche there. The choice is yours.

The cost in terms of time, money, and expertise varies massively. You could go from hiring a single developer on freelancer.com or upwork.com, who could easily create an online calorie calculator app. Or you could work with a top-level development team that you hire full-time to create an app that counts calories burned using the latest features in wearable technology or implants. The first option might cost you a few hundred dollars, whereas the second option could be hundreds of thousands and more – probably more.

I'm a big fan of software. I created DistroList.app as a software solution to the manual work I did for myself and others. Bookkeeping software is another great example of where software can stand in place of or facilitate a complex or repetitive process.

The best part about software is that once you reach the point where you have a minimal viable product (MVP), you can switch your focus to sales and start benefiting from the high-profit margins usually associated with software.

#5 Information Products

This option is, by far, one of the most start-up-friendly ways to serve your niche. Not only are information products low-cost to produce, but you can generally benefit from a very high-profit margin, exceptionally high in many cases.

Take this book, for example. If you set aside the monumental cost of the time it took me to write it (it took me ages), the unit cost to print the book is very low. This book has a high-profit margin even with a relatively low retail price. A book is one example of an information product that you could create in response to the questions you receive from your survey.

Now, consider the other types of information products out there. I could think about charging a few thousand dollars for a home study program that deep dives into the concepts shared in this book. Much like the book, once I create the program material itself, the unit cost of delivering that program is very low. I could charge even more for live and in-person workshops, where over a few intensive days, I coach in a group setting the buildout of your offer and find you your DistroAgents to help get you selling and making money immediately. Now, consider one-on-one consulting. And yes, in case you were wondering, I do all these. For more information, check out DistroChannels.com.

New term alert! I'm going to start referring to influencers, businesses, and any other person, place, or thing that is considered an active distribution partner as DistroAgents from here on out. And later, when you have a bunch of DistroAgents working for you, I'm going to call that your DistroNetwork. Notice the theme here... DistroAgents, DistroNetwork, DistroTeams, DistroLeaders, and just wait until you reach DistroUtopia! Did I mention DistroList... anyway, moving on.

Information products are, by nature, highly niche-specific. You, or better still, you and other known and respected names in the market can package your collective experience and expertise into information products like books, courses, seminars, coaching, and consulting. It's a fantastic option to get to work on immediately and serve your niche with whatever it is they need.

#6 Service Offering

If information products are the DIY option (do it yourself), then services are the D4U options (done for you). You can almost always provide a done-for-you service offer for a niche audience. Unless your audience requests solutions to problems in heavily regulated fields, such as finance or legal services, you can usually align a specific outcome as a service with whatever is being requested.

Professional services, from bookkeeping and recruitment to air conditioning maintenance and cleaning services, are general examples. But that's not what I'm talking about here. I want you to get really specific to your niche. I'm literally referring to your service offer as you fulfilling outcomes for the top most-requested things that come back from your survey. You are telling your audience that you listened and created a done-for-you option for them to address their needs. My first businesses were mostly service orientated, and they all made good money.

While writing this book and simultaneously developing my software app, DistroList.app, I followed the same 4 steps. The survey responses I received centered around people wanting pre-built DistroLists organized by category and paying to have distribution networks cultivated for them, including handling the recruitment and negotiation side of things. So sure enough, that's one of the services my company provides. And yes, that sounds like another shameless plug. It is. Sorry, not sorry. You can find out more about my services at DistroChannels.com or try my software app, DistroList. app, for free.

However, one thing to remember about offering a service is that the production and consumption of that service happen at the same time. By that, I mean the service itself is literally the effort, output, and result of a person, machine, or software working on a task. The quality of that outcome is immediately visible, so you'd better make sure you can execute it well. Otherwise, you may not be asked to do it (whatever it was) again.

This is where collaborating with other experts in your submarket really pays off, literally. Having the ability to tap into the collective experience and resources of others to deliver on a promise is invaluable. By the way, a promise is exactly what a service is. So, choosing to collaborate can mean all the difference in whether you can deliver on what you promise or not.

Decision Time

So, which direction are you going to go? Do you want to offer more than one type of product or service? And are you going to collaborate with others in your submarket? Or are you going to go it alone? You could bundle more than one type together. Part of the bundle could be something you created independently, and another could be something you collaborated on.

The truth is, whichever direction you go at this stage is fine, provided you followed these steps. If you have, that means you did your research, know what your niche audience wants, and know who your hot buyers are! You can reasonably predict your sales based on the number of people who responded to your survey. I usually ballpark at 30% conversion, assuming you created a sensible offer. This conversion rate is higher because they told you what they wanted and are *hot* buyers.

As the old saying goes, the honor is in the dollar, so whether you own 25%, 50%, or 100% of a business, your success is really determined by how much money you make. That means the price of your offer is also an important factor.

Pricing

Saying, "You've got to price it right," is like opening Pandora's box. A lot of know-it-alls out there can bore you to death with the art and science of pricing. There's a ton of theory and a lot of opinions, too. Pick up any business book or Google the subject, and you'll be inundated with pricing philosophy, pulling you in all sorts of directions. At the same time, you'll also see plenty of warnings that the wrong pricing could kill your offer, but the right pricing could increase your sales through the roof. The troublesome thing is that most of those warnings are true.

There are theories for how to price to maximize your profit and also plenty for maximizing your sales. You can deep dive into the art and science of price skimming strategies, penetration pricing strategies, status quo pricing, value-based pricing, and so on. The list is long, but don't worry. I won't bore you with descriptions – you have Google for that.

At this stage in your business life cycle, it's important to keep things as simple as possible. Your goal right now should be focused on pricing in such a way that gives you a margin of profit large enough to cover your production and advertising costs and leave you with a healthy profit. In other words, is it worth putting in the effort to sell it?

That brings us down to 2 simple factors:

1. Having a big profit margin as a percentage and
2. Having it priced high enough for that *percentage* to be a meaningful amount of money.

With those factors in mind, I recommend going with what's known as the 3X rule. You are essentially trying to mark your offer up at least 3X the cost of production. This means that in percentages, you'll end up with margins hovering around 70%. It's actually approximately 66.67%, but I'm rounding up. And when it comes to the pricing at this stage, in terms of money, I think you should price it as high as you can get away with.

Let me explain that quickly. A 70% margin on a $10 offer is not equal to a 70% margin on a $100 offer. The $10 offer only generates a $7 gross profit, whereas the $100 product generates a $70 gross profit. That's a big difference, especially when it comes to how much you can pay out in advertising and incentives. The amount of money in the margin matters every bit as much as the percentage, if not more.

Pro Tip

Don't waste your time trying to get an advanced degree in pricing. Keep it simple and start by using the 3X rule to price your offer. This will yield a big profit margin, giving you enough cushion to play with your cost variables, such as how much to pay advertisers and offer as incentives.

We covered a lot in this part, but the steps I shared are truly what I know to be the easiest way to find out what to sell while also letting you know exactly who to sell to. If you are still not totally convinced that you can put together a profitable business, go back and reread this section of the book. I know you can do this!

Having equipped you with the skills to construct irresistible offers in Part 2, a crucial cornerstone for building a profitable business, it's time to shift our focus to Part 3: Accelerate Growth, Drive Up Sales. This section is geared toward accelerating the growth of your business by showing you how to seriously boost sales and scale your distribution networks to a whole new level.

Action Plan

Analyzing Survey Results

- **Evaluate responses**: Analyze the survey results to understand what your submarket truly desires, regardless of the response rate.

Deciding on the Product or Service

- **Choose your path**: Decide whether to:
  - Create and develop your own product or service.
  - Sell another company's products or services.
  - Combine both approaches.

Creating Your Offer

- **Identify top questions**: From your survey results, pick the top three questions or those with significant response rates.

- **Transform questions into benefit statements**: Convert these questions into statements that illustrate the benefits of your potential offer.

Options for Product Creation

- **Engage with DistroList contacts**: Collaborate with businesses or influencers in your DistroList to create an offer.

- **Consider private labeling**: Explore private labeling for physical products or software.

- **Evaluate OEM opportunities**: Look into Original Equipment Manufacturer options for unique product creation.

- **Develop digital products**: Think about creating digital or software products.

- **Create information products**: Develop books, courses, or seminars based on your expertise.

- **Offer service solutions**: Provide services that directly address the needs highlighted in your survey.

Pricing Your Offer

- **Adopt the 3X rule**: Aim for a pricing strategy that marks up your offer at least 3X the cost of production, targeting a 70% margin.

- **Price as high as feasible**: Set prices high enough to ensure your profit margins are meaningful.

Part 3

ACCELERATE GROWTH, DRIVE UP SALES

"Cultivate a powerful distribution network, unleashing your business' full potential"

The Epiphany

People often talk about the entrepreneur's runway. Picture an airplane runway where the end of the runway is the edge of a cliff. If you want to fly your airplane, you need to accelerate your plane down the runway and take off before you fall off the edge of that cliff.

In this metaphor, the plane is your startup business, and the runway is the amount of money, and therefore time, you have before your startup takes off and becomes profitable. If you run out of runway and you haven't taken off, that means you're out of money and can no longer continue with your venture.

Whether you have a long or short runway, the problem with that metaphor is that it sounds so clinical, as if the entrepreneur is financially removed from the risks of failure. When I hear people use that expression, I feel like it only really applies when you're using someone else's money.

When I think of entrepreneurship, I tend to think of it as jumping off a cliff and building an airplane on the way down! It's a far more accurate description, especially when you're using your own money. Think about it. First you need a lot of courage and faith in yourself to take the leap. You need to believe, on a very deep level, that you can pull it off because if you don't make it, you're broke, right?

Next, you need to be comfortable in a state of chaos because once you jump off that cliff, the ground is coming at you fast. If you move slowly, you're dead. You must use your ingenuity and problem-solving skills to put together a plane in freefall. The stakes are high – you either live or die. If you don't assemble the entire plane and get it running, you die. And not just for you either. It's the same outcome for everyone else you persuaded to jump with you, too.

Everything I teach you to do in this book is about how to get into business and start making money immediately. In Part 1: Empower Yourself, Earn Instantly, I showed you how to sell that offer super fast. To preserve precious resources like time and money, I showed you how to get started at low-to-no cost, and I've shown you how to pool your resources to include help from other people in the form of collaborations and joint ventures.

What I'm about to share with you is something I learned before everything I shared in Part 2: Create Irresistible Offers, On Demand. In hindsight, I wish I had discovered it afterwards because it works best when you already have a solid foundation. By that, I mean you know exactly what your niche is, and you have a great offer available, which is something you know your market wants or needs. This secret is all about how to sell fast, efficiently, and at high volume.

Back in 2010, I was desperately looking for ways to save my dying business. I had recently quit my safe-and-stable job to pursue my dream of becoming a successful entrepreneur. Unfortunately, as is the case with many startup ideas, my business was already turning out to be a monumental failure. And I had only been in business for a few months. I had no more money. My bank accounts were empty, and I was deep into overdrafts. I couldn't pay my rent and barely had enough to feed myself. Life was looking bleak and all-around depressing with no lifelines in sight.

I had spent the first few months – and what would seem to be the last few months – in this startup working desperately to find new deals. I had started a consulting business in the recruitment and headhunting sector. This meant I spent my days either glued to the phone or rushing to meetings trying to find companies that would agree to pay me a fee to recruit for some of their more specialized job openings.

I had spent whatever money I had on various advertising options, from online ads to print media marketing strategies. I was burning through my available cash, time, and energy fast. I spent 90% of my time trying to drum up business and only 10% of my time serving clients. With all my money tied up in advertising, I couldn't afford to hire any help. Does that sound familiar?

My days were so intense that I barely had any breathing room between tasks. I had zero personal time with no hope of achieving that ever-coveted work-life balance. I desperately needed a solution to fix my cash flow problem, and I needed it fast. I remember scouring the internet for solutions and a quick fix to my problem. But all I could find were online marketing agencies and lead generation companies promising to send *hot* leads for hefty upfront fees. There were a lot of free and paid courses on do-it-yourself complex pay-per-click advertising options among a mountain of other choices. I felt overwhelmed and deflated, and I did not have the time or money required to learn and experiment with any of them. I was ready to throw in the towel.

I was at a breaking point, ready to admit to my peers, colleagues, family, and friends that I could not make it on my own. And without some kind of divine, magical intervention, I would be throwing in the towel and quitting. I needed help. But I wasn't looking for financial assistance like a handout or for someone to stand in place of the credit cards I had already burned through.

What I wanted – and needed – was for someone to help me achieve my business goals. I'm not referring to mentorship, either. Even though I definitely needed some solid business advice and guidance, that would not have saved my business or paid the bills in the short term.

Around that time, I was speaking to a good friend and long-time client of mine, Dani, who owned a corporate training company. At the time, he needed help recruiting business development executives, a fancy title for salespeople, to help sell his training programs to corporate clients in London.

In our talk, he explained that he was a little hesitant about hiring a salesperson because the truth was, he had never needed one before nor had to manage salespeople. He'd also never had to set up the advertising campaigns or program the software to drive in sales leads and keep track of sales workflows.

This surprised and confused me as to how he had been selling his training programs. I was expecting him to tell me about an elaborate online marketing funnel from which I could probably take a few pointers that would help me with my own client acquisition troubles. But what he said next hit me like a ton of bricks and triggered the epiphany I had been waiting for!

He explained that up until that point he had never had sales staff or put together any special online advertising funnels, and that ALL his corporate clients came from word-of-mouth referrals. That was it. Referrals. Not exactly groundbreaking information, but bear with me…

He went on to say that, unfortunately, he wasn't generating enough business, and that it's hard to control or scale up the number of referrals you get. After all, the only incentive or control measure in place was to offer a referral fee. After that, it was just a waiting game.

His plan now, like a lot of businesses in the same position, was to hire salespeople, and then put together an elaborate marketing campaign that would funnel potential leads into a customer relationship management (CRM) software system and have his salesperson(s) call, follow up, nurture potential clients, and eventually win business. Then, he could deliver his training program, and the process would repeat. Referrals, he hoped, would organically increase over time.

Then – and this is the part where the proverbial bricks hit me – he jokingly said that he wished he could cut that process in half, and simply have me recruit referral partners for him.

That was it! What he had just told me changed my entire outlook. It was like looking at business through a completely new lens. Why was this a joke to him, I thought. I'm a recruiter, a headhunter, and it's my job to find people. Finding referral partners is exactly what I should be doing for him. And for myself, too.

All I needed to do was find the people who had influence over the customers he wanted to sell to. When I found those people, all I needed to do was give them a good enough reason to refer, recommend, and sell for him.

For Dani, it meant he could focus on delivering the best training for his clients. For me, it was the lifeline I was looking for. The help I needed was from the people who had direct access to the customer groups I was targeting. If they had a relationship with the customers I wanted to sell to, they could help finish the job I was struggling to do. All I needed was to give them a good enough reason to sell for me. And, what better incentive is there other than money?

I could simply cut someone into the profit I would make. It was a win-win. Collaborating with people and businesses in this way helped me sell faster and recover financially within weeks!

I couldn't believe no one had told me about this or why I had not discovered this painfully obvious solution earlier. Working with someone else in my industry to get the job done faster seems like such a natural thing to do.

When I thought about it, there were so many times when I have tapped into someone else's knowledge, experience, or access to complete a task and split the reward. I'm pretty sure if you look at your own life, you'll see that you've done this also, in one way or another.

Have you ever asked a friend to help you sell something? And that if they sold it, you would give them a portion of the profit or some other reward? I remember moving apartments one time and was rushing to sell some of my furniture. I asked a friend to help me sell my sofa and promised them a cut of the selling price if they found a buyer. I was leveraging their network and sales skills to get the job done, and they were rewarded for their effort when the sofa sold.

Well, that transaction is one of the most natural things we do to make life easier for ourselves when we need to sell something. Distribution channels work similarly – teaming up with partners who have the right connections and audience to boost your sales and share the rewards.

The New Step

This realization marks the beginning of a business strategy I promptly and proudly labeled the getting-other-people-to-sell-my-stuff-for-me strategy. Of course, this approach is quite well-known and not something I invented. It also has a far more sensible label.

Today, we use labels like influencer marketing, strategic partnering, introducer networking, affiliate marketing, network marketing, and joint venturing to name a few. These collaborations are some of the best ways to sell fast, build your business, and make more money!

I replicated this method in the recruitment sector and investment world and saw huge success in my earnings and how fast my business grew. Focusing on working with what I describe as the meatware (people) behind the hardware (businesses) was superior to learning any new marketing, sales, or traffic hacks.

Speaking of trending labels and buzzwords, I'd like to point out that there are and will always be people and agencies proclaiming that they are experts in those fields, attempting to capitalize on the latest trend. For example, labels like influencer marketing and social media marketing are so new that nobody (not even me) could truly be an expert. Unfortunately for me, I had to learn this the hard way as I usually do…

My experience when working with those people and agencies proclaiming themselves as social media and influencer marketing experts only went so far. I found that all they could do was create a few Facebook, Instagram, and X pages and ask me for updates that they would periodically post on my behalf while blowing through thousands of dollars on social media ads.

And the people and agencies promoting their expertise with influencer marketing charged astronomical service fees to match my brand with relevant influencers but, frankly, had no idea how to recruit, retain, or even manage those relationships.

What these people didn't recognize was that to influence through social media properly required a much deeper understanding of what constitutes a good campaign. Simply posting to a few fan pages and paying a few social media personalities for shoutouts was just the first layer of its potential influence and impact.

To be successful with any of these collaborations, whether it's working with influencers, affiliates, introducers, or any other business or person, you need to understand how leverage works. That little secret underpins everything. In fact, understanding leverage is the key to increasing sales conversions and money in general.

Let's break it down. Most people get paid for the hours they work, but with leverage, you can make way more money in way less time. Imagine making $100,000 in a year by working around $50 per hour for 40 hours a week.

But here's the exciting part. With leverage, you can level up and make $100,000 in a month or even a single day! Sounds amazing, right? So instead of going it alone, you could team up with influencers, affiliates, and other business owners that have a massive audience and following or even businesses with products and services that have huge customer lists.

By collaborating with them, you tap into their audience and significantly benefit from the power of their influence. Leverage is everything. Once you understand its magic, you'll see that it's quite simple, and you can become really good at it!

If we go back to influencer marketing, for example, successful leveraging would require that you concentrate on creating value for a target audience group. If you find and engage the right influencers who share the same interests, problems, or values as your target audience, the interactions with your potential customers will be more authentic. By this, I mean that the information or message you are trying to convey will be given a personal voice that you can focus on leveraging by making it insightful and engaging.

If you followed the steps I outlined in Part 2: Create Irresistible Offers, On Demand, you chose your niche, defined your target audience groups, built your DistroList, and created lists of your potential influencers and other DistroAgents.

Every person, place, or thing you put in your DistroList will have its own distribution channel for its respective audience group. Your influencers will have their audiences on one or more of their preferred social media platforms, and others will have podcasts with lots of subscribers. You'll also have businesses and bloggers with substantial email lists. In many cases, you'll find that most will have more than one distribution channel, too. Are you starting to see the power of this strategy yet?

If you can recruit just 10 of those distinct partners, where each one had lists of tens of thousands of people each, you could get your offer in front of 100,000+ of your ideal audience groups. What if you could recruit 50, 100, or even 1,000+ like I did? You could get your offer in front of millions of your ideal audience and, more importantly, have your offer actively endorsed by the person, place, or thing whose audience group has an established level of trust and faith.

Remember what I said about leverage? Well, imagine the amount of leverage you have when you build a successful DistroNetwork like this! Shifting the workload to other people, who are much better positioned to sell than you are, is a monumental benefit. It's almost like you're hiring a huge sales team to sell your stuff except that when you collaborate this way, you are not paying them to clock in and work at it.

Instead, it's pay-on-performance so that you're usually only paying them a commission for a completed sale or specific action. The difference here lies in the nature of the collaboration, such as where an influencer endorses your offer as a shoutout to a highly targeted audience. Instead of hiring them as regular employees, this approach operates on various models. Some involve paying them upfront for their endorsement, while others operate on a pay-on-performance basis. The risk is on them, but if they make a sale, both of you benefit.

Let me put it another way. You could literally have zero ad spend, while at the same time having ads for your offer flooding an entire market. That means no more paying for expensive advertising and hoping for conversions. You no longer need to become a master of SEO or SEM, and you don't need to build your own highly engaged social media audiences or email lists. You are mobilizing an army of boots-on-the-ground individuals as your distribution partners who will promote your offer with their own preferred method of marketing.

Some might be targeting their audiences with SEO, SEM, Banner Ads on their websites, and direct email marketing. They might pick up the phone and call their clients, or they may even host an event where they pitch your offer to a live audience. Others might do it through conversations they're having inside their podcasts, within their YouTube videos, or engaging audiences on their Instagram, Facebook, TikTok, and other social media. Some might use a combination of these methods. The silver lining is that you are leveraging their expertise and reputation with their market and chosen advertising method, and you only pay them after they make a sale or some other specific outcome. Amazing, right?

But there's one other factor to recognize – they don't actually need you. You need them. To recruit DistroAgents, you need a plan before you approach them and ask them to promote your product or service.

The good news is the plan consists of 4 very simple steps. And if you've been following my guidance, you'll already have a huge number of distribution partners ready.

For me to do this, I followed 4 steps:

1. Decide what you are going to offer.
2. Establish the collaboration type.
3. Determine how you will recruit them.
4. Figure out how you're going to manage and improve performance.

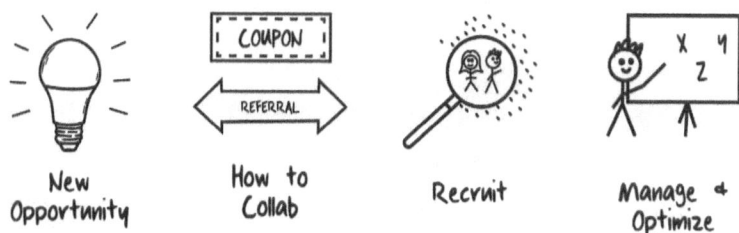

New
Opportunity

How to
Collab

Recruit

Manage &
Optimize

Step 1: What Is the New Opportunity?

One of the most common questions I come across when people are setting up their distribution channels is about how to position their new opportunity. They want to know how to ensure it's desirable and provides enough incentive for their DistroAgents to start and continue promoting them.

There are 2 things to consider when motivating your DistroAgents:

1. How much will you pay them to promote and sell for you?
2. Does your offer complement what they do?

Pro Tip

Like I said before, money talks, so new opportunities are not the time to be cheap. When positioning new opportunities for DistroAgents, if you can afford it, I suggest paying them an initial fee to get started while also offering above-average commissions. For added traction and to maximize ROI, make sure that your offer complements what they already do, which will make selling your opportunity easier.

The good news is that if you followed my recipe in Part 2, then you are ahead of the game. Even if you marginally followed it, you will have something that has enough profit margin for you to offer a decent financial incentive and is desirable for your DistroAgents' audience groups.

Let's talk about the money first.

Most people I speak to about this assume they should be trying to pay as little as possible so that they can keep more profit in the business and for themselves. But actually, the opposite is true. You should be positioning your offer as a fantastic opportunity that pays extremely well. Think about how you can pay out the most money.

The philosophy of being able to pay out a lot of money as an incentive underpins my rationale behind the 3X rule. If you marked your offer up at least 3X the production cost, you should be able to pay out at least 30% of the total price of your offer. That does not mean 30% is all you should be willing to pay out. That is the minimum. I have sometimes paid out as much as 70%. However, I think 30% is a sweet spot, and what most people consider an above-average commission.

I'm going to keep this focused on what's known as pay-on-performance, which basically means we are only interested in paying out money when a sale is completed. You might be thinking that if you follow the 3X rule, it would allow for enough profit to give you a big enough budget to pay for a campaign upfront. If you thought that, you're not wrong. There will be plenty of opportunities where you will want to pay your DistroAgents for broadcasting your sales message. You'll have options from simple influencer shoutouts, email ads, and banner ads to more carefully integrated branding, engagement-focused, and direct response campaigns.

Considering where you are in your business life cycle, I want to focus on low-cost to no-cost options first. Once your business takes off and more money is available, we can then move toward campaigns where we combine upfront and performance-based payment structures.

With performance-based payouts, there are two ways to go. The first is where you pay out a percentage of the sale, and the second is paying out a flat fee on each sale made. For example, if your offer is $100, you could pay out 30% ($30), or you could assign a flat fee of $30 per sale.

It's important to make this distinction so that your DistroAgents are clear about how much they can make. For example, you may think it's a good idea to run a 50% off holiday special deal around Christmas to bring in more customers. You could even justify the reduced income per sale with the fact that you intend to offer the newly acquired customer with something else – either immediately after or later – that would be more profitable to you.

While that might be a great idea, it's not so great for your DistroAgents who would earn a lot less per sale throughout the holiday period. Say they were being paid 30% on a $100 offer. For a 50% off holiday special, their earnings would drop from $30 to $15 per sale. That's a big financial hit, and many of them would probably stop promoting your offer and go with something else that pays better.

Consider how this dynamic changes if your DistroAgent payout was a $30 flat fee per sale. That would mean that even if you dropped your sale price to 50% off, 70% off, or even for free, your DistroAgent would still earn $30 per completed transaction. Not only are they more likely to continue to promote your offer, but they may actually push even harder during those periods.

At one point, I paid out a flat fee of $30 for every new free trial signup to my website. I remember having a small panic attack when I worked with one influencer. She simply posted the video and requested her following to sign up for the free trial. I had 1,000+ people in less than one hour! I quickly stopped the campaign thinking my plan had backfired and I'd wasted $30,000.

Yet, it turned out to be quite the opposite. Once the trial ended 14 days later, roughly 30% of those signups stayed and paid the $97 monthly fee. That brought in the same amount of money I had paid out.

Comparing the cost of the signups ($30,000) with the revenue generated ($29,100), you see that the revenue just about covered the cost. So, despite my initial panic, the campaign turned out to be a success, and I didn't waste $30,000. And let's not forget that many of those paying customers continued their subscription for at least one more month and paid the $97 charge again. But I didn't have to pay an additional $30 signup fee to the influencer.

In effect, I pretty much broke even on my initial outlay within the first month, which was fantastic. I acquired around 300 new people who are now experiencing my stuff and paying me, without losing a penny to get them. From that point on, anything else they purchased from me, however small or large, would be all profit.

What does this mean for you? It means I want you to offer your DistroAgents amazing commissions. Do not shy away from paying above-average performance fees. I mentioned this before, and I'll say it again. **You need them – they don't need you**. You are selling the prospective DistroAgent on reasons why they should promote your thing. When thinking about how much you want to pay out, take a moment to remember why you are trying to work with them in the first place. Think about how much more likely people are to buy something based on a recommendation from someone they know, like, and trust (your DistroAgent) as opposed to somebody they don't know (you).

Put differently, if you could pitch your offer to 50 people per day, 5 days per week for an entire month, you would put your offer in front of 1,000 potential buyers. Most people consider that a pretty good start because that's how most people operate.

But let's instead say you approached 100 potential DistroAgents and ended up with only 3 who agreed to promote your offer. Say the first had an audience of 20,000, the second 8,000, and the third 12,000. When they promote your offer, your sales message would be immediately in front of 40,000 potential buyers.

Even more conservatively, say that 2 of these DistroAgents somehow forgot to promote your thing, and only the 1 with the smallest audience of 8,000 promoted it... that's still much better than the original 1,000 you could have pitched to over an entire month. And by the way, pitching 50 people individually per day for a month in today's world is crazy. Aside from being very inefficient, that's a fast track to burnout.

I know this because I started out in direct sales and selling one person at a time can take its toll on you, especially when the ticket price is not very high. Remember, you want to work to live, not live to work, right? One DistroAgent could earn you thousands if not millions of dollars. So, pay generously, and bring as many DistroAgents on board as you can. This is by far the fastest way to build and grow your business.

The other thing I believe you need to factor in is whether your offer complements what they do. It should uplift the value of their offer as opposed to something directly conflicting with theirs or acts as a substitute for their thing.

Think about it this way. It's not likely you could collaborate with a DistroAgent if you have a product that stands in place of theirs. The same is true if your offer is something that conflicts with their values. For example, a fitness influencer, who promotes a vegan diet and has their own line of vegan protein shakes, would probably not want to collaborate with you if your business specializes in home-delivered premium steaks. You'd obviously be better off looking for an influencer promoting a carnivore diet. I hope you see the point I'm trying to make.

In Part 2: Create Irresistible Offers, On Demand, you focused on creating your own niche offer, not choosing an existing niche. Following the steps in that section helped you create a unique offer with a higher probability of being paired with other niche offers within that submarket. Naturally, some will directly conflict like the example above, but there's usually a lot of opportunity for complementary pairings, even if it's not immediately obvious. You see... not many products or services are used in a vacuum, meaning there's usually something needed before or after. It may require being creative to make your offer fit, but this helps the collaboration seem like a match made in heaven.

I'll say this another way because it's extremely important. Even though it looks like you're targeting an audience full of cold prospects where no one knows you or has never bought anything from you in the past, they're actually not cold prospects at all. Granted, they may be cold to you, but because they've either engaged, consumed, or purchased something from your DistroAgent before, it actually makes them warm or perhaps even hot buyers!

Provided your offer complements the DistroAgent's product or their values, you should be able to collaborate. Plus, if you offer amazing commissions, you'll be presenting a very enticing opportunity that will be very difficult for a prospective DistroAgent to pass up.

Action Plan

Positioning Your Opportunity

- **Figure out the payment structure for DistroAgents**: Establish the payment structure for your DistroAgents, including any initial fees and commissions.

- **Be sure to align offers with DistroAgents' products/ services**: Your offer should add value to what the DistroAgents already offer or complement what they do.

Fine-Tune Your Offer

- **Provide lucrative commissions**: Offer above-average commissions to incentivize DistroAgents.

- **Use the 3X rule for pricing**: Use the 3X rule so that your pricing allows for significant commission payouts.

- **Choose between a percentage or flat fee**: Decide whether to pay DistroAgents a percentage or a flat fee for each sale.

- **Clarify payout terms during promotions**: Ensure DistroAgents understand how their earnings are calculated, especially during discount periods.

By following these steps, you can effectively position your new opportunity in a way that appeals to your potential DistroAgents, ensuring it is both desirable and provides a strong incentive for them to promote your products or services.

■ Step 2: How Will You Collaborate?

The offer you present is important. That takes care of the *why*, but now you need to cover the *how*. In this case, the *how* relates to the next thing your DistroAgent will naturally want to know, which is whether this collaboration will work and more importantly, how and when will they be compensated. They may not admit this, but it will be on their minds.

Selling someone on the offer is one thing. But running a smooth operation to deliver on what you promise and ensuring there's a good infrastructure and system in place to support the collaboration is another thing entirely. For instance, customers complaining to your DistroAgents about late deliveries are forgivable. Complaints about product defects are forgivable. Even complaints about sending the wrong product are forgivable! But nothing, and I mean nothing, will kill a collaboration faster than not paying their expected commission at the agreed time. It doesn't matter if you forget to pay, didn't know you needed to pay, or paid the wrong amount. This is an area of mishaps and mixups that sit firmly in the realm of the unforgivable. I promise I'm not over-exaggerating.

I see so many people gloss over this critical component. Bringing people on board without a system in place is a recipe for disaster, like biting off more than you can chew. I know people out there who will tell you that it's a "good problem to have" if things get a little messy and you don't know how much to pay people because your campaign had a ton of sales and made a lot of money. Well, they are wrong. They've probably never run multiple campaigns or managed successful distribution channels. They're idiots. Don't listen to them. It's not a good problem to have.

Learning things the hard way and making mistakes is the origin from which most of my advice comes from. Sure, for some things, making mistakes and learning through failure is crucial for permanently changing habits or discovering something new. But then other things can simply be passed on as good advice without some earth-shattering reason why it's important. This is one of those things.

I once had a mixup where I paid the wrong amount of money to two of my DistroAgents. I mixed up their amounts when wiring the money. I immediately realized what I'd done and contacted them both. The problem was solved in under 24 hours, and each of my DistroAgents had the correct payment. Everyone was happy. Wrong! It just so happened that these two DistroAgents were new recruits, and this was their first payment. It was impossible for them to turn a blind eye to the blunder, and it haunted me for a year at least.

People talk. People like to complain about stuff. Word will spread despite how compartmentalized or isolated you thought something was. I ended up having new prospective DistroAgents, and many existing ones, making backhanded comments here and there about having to double-check their commission payments – as if they wouldn't check anyway.

I started seeing comments on message boards saying similar things like, "Great product, it sells really well but can be a hassle to get paid." Or even snarkier like "Would be a fantastic product if only they paid on time." These people weren't even my DistroAgents.

They were online trolls who had no affiliation with my business besides fanning the flames and boosting issues that have nothing to do with them. (I'm sure they like to consider themselves community watchdogs, but they're just trolls).

There was nothing I could do about any of it. Who knows how much business I lost because of that seemingly isolated mixup. How big of a loss could 1 DistroAgent be to me – $10,000, $100,000, $1M, $10M? I have no idea but never want to risk losing or deterring a DistroAgent from a blunder like that ever again.

So perhaps that was an earth-shattering reason why having a sales tracking and payment system underpinning your collaboration is important – at least from a business sense. Still need convincing?

Think about how you would feel if you landed a new job, worked hard all month, and on payday, the company forgot to pay, paid the wrong amount, or said they needed to delay paying you because they fudged the numbers and are trying to work everything out. I'm sure you'd be very unhappy. It's no different with collaborations. You have a deal in place with your DistroAgent, and when they deliver, they will expect you to hold up your end of the deal.

Here is one simple way you can go about setting things up so that you have a professional "easy to see how it works" platform for your offer. This way, you can confidently start introducing your *why* and *how* to prospective DistroAgents.

Set Up an Affiliate Program

This is the easiest way to work with anyone on your DistroList. You can recruit hundreds or even thousands of affiliates with no risk. I use affiliate platforms for all my DistroAgents, who are essentially acting as external sales agents, introducers, and other referral partners. They are all essentially different versions of the same thing, and affiliate platforms can support most of these agreement types.

I've seen a lot of success embedding affiliate marketing software like LeadDyno and Tapfiliate into my businesses. Regardless of the platform you choose, you'll notice that the software depends on your DistroAgents to promote your offer, and you agree on paying a specific partner a commission if they initiate a sale. The system tracks everything automatically, and you only pay out if they actually sell something. This setup even works with introducer and referral partners who typically operate offline. Affiliate platforms can track deals against specific DistroAgents using coupon codes, promo codes, referral IDs, and other unique identifiers over and above its typical email and digital footprint tracking capabilities.

When an Affiliate Program Isn't Enough

Having said that, if you believe your collaboration is going to be more complex, an affiliate platform may not be all you need. This could apply to anything. For example, you could have a very high ticket offer where sales need to be done in person and require lots of paperwork and even regulatory reporting before closing a deal. Maybe you're selling real estate, cars, yachts, or jewelry. Or perhaps it's a tailor-made business consulting service. Whatever the case, increased complexity requires a more thought-out system, more people power, and support tools. These collaborations fall into the realm of strategic partnerships and joint ventures (JVs).

It could be the case that you might want to co-create a unique offer that is exclusive to a specific DistroAgent. You may want to do a joint/co-branded campaign or embed your offer into different areas of someone else's funnel, such as an upsell or a downsell. What if you wanted to specify upfront payments or performance payments that are not tied to completed sales, rendering an affiliate platform useless. You may want to reward your DistroAgents under a tiered or sliding scale structure for achieving a certain number of shares, comments, responses to a survey, or other non-monetary deliverable.

Tracking many of these will have you turning to simple spreadsheets, notes, and emails. But there are software platforms, such as Zoho and Salesforce, that can automate or assist with some of these manual processes.

I personally started out doing things manually, and it worked well enough at the time. I was selling real estate, which is high-ticket as products go. Plus, they have a lengthy closing procedure. My spreadsheet listed all the sales by DistroAgent. These DistroAgents, which included external sales agents, introducers, influencers (as in social media personalities), referral agents, and website owners worldwide. They emailed or phoned in their client's details before forwarding the client to us. Then, they would keep in close contact throughout the process. I later upgraded to a sales customer relationship management (CRM) tool that automated or assisted with aspects like drip emails, reporting, better organization, and more security, but it was still a manual setup.

However, when I created offers that were sold online, my DistroAgents were directing their buyer groups to web pages I had set up. This required an affiliate management and payment platform to keep things running smoothly.

For some collaborations, you may want (or be required) to track sales and make payments manually or use software that automates and simplifies tracking and payments. Or you may want a combination of manual and automated systems. Whatever you decide, make sure you set it up before you start recruiting anyone.

Pro Tip

I created DistroList.app, a platform designed to connect you with the persons, places, and things that already have access to your target audience. One of the features of this platform is the option to showcase your offer as an affiliate opportunity within the internal marketplace. This means other DistroAgents can choose to promote your product through their network and generate immediate sales. They might already have a pre-cultivated, well-established distribution network that aligns with your target buyer demographic, which means promoting your offer is a no brainer. Head over to DistroList.app and start a free trial to kickstart the process!

Action Plan

Action Steps for Collaborating and Compensating
DistroAgents

- **Understand DistroAgents' concerns**: Recognize that DistroAgents will be concerned about the effectiveness of the collaboration and, importantly, how and when they will be paid.

- **Consider the complexity of collaborations**: If your offer involves high-ticket items or complex sales processes, a simple affiliate system may not be enough. In these cases, consider using CRM tools like Zoho or Salesforce.

- **Offer clear financial incentives**: Be transparent about the compensation structure, whether it's a percentage of sales or a flat fee, and ensure it is attractive enough to motivate DistroAgents.

- **Communicate clearly with prospective DistroAgents**: When approaching potential DistroAgents, explain both the opportunity and the support system in place.

- **Set up before recruitment**: Make sure your tracking and payment systems are in place before starting to recruit DistroAgents.

- **Prioritize timely payments**: Avoid collaboration issues by guaranteeing timely and accurate payments to your DistroAgents. Mishandling payments can quickly damage relationships and your reputation.

- **Implement a reliable sales tracking and payment system**: Set up a system to track sales made by DistroAgents and manage payments. This could be through an affiliate platform or a more manual system for complex collaborations.

- **Set up an affiliate program**: Consider using affiliate marketing platforms like LeadDyno or Tapfiliate. These platforms can manage affiliate relationships, track sales, and handle payments automatically.

By following these steps, you can effectively set up a collaboration system with your DistroAgents, ensuring smooth operation, reliable compensation, and mutually beneficial relationships.

Step 3: How Are You Going to Recruit Them?

In Part 2: Create Irresistible Offers, On Demand, you identified your ideal customer, and I showed you how to find those persons, places, and things that have and hold their attention.

At this stage, if you don't already know who your ideal customer is or where your buyer groups are, you probably did not follow my concepts. In that case, it will be much harder for you to take action. Let me say that differently. If you have not read Part 2, go back and cover that section first and actually do the work. It will pay off. I promise!

For those who know their ideal customer and who already holds their attention, you will now learn how easy it is to get your opportunity in front of them and pull them into your sales funnels.

Some of what I'm about to explain was covered previously, but now I'll give you much more detail in a step-by-step walkthrough to find, recruit, and start selling your opportunity. What matters most here is your DistroList. Think about all the persons, places, and things that have the attention and, therefore, influence over your target buyers.

What websites do they go to? What social media personalities do they follow, and what blogs do they read? Do they listen to podcasts, and do they spend their time on YouTube channels? You can look into the products and services they already purchase and the companies that created or sold those things. Imagine how valuable their customer lists could be to your business. It would be like striking gold.

Think about other types of list owners. How about the newsletters people sign up for? Does your audience go to conferences or other events? These places have attendee and delegate lists, too. What about the books they read? Could you reach out to book authors? They are thought leaders, after all, and will have a highly engaged niche audience. What other things are your ideal buyers searching for online? What games do they play? What apps and software do they use?

These are all relevant questions. You'll also find that many of these questions will result in audience overlap, like where an influencer personality will have a blog, Instagram, podcast, and YouTube channel. But each person, place, or thing is an attention magnet. They all have the power to sway the decisions of your target customer.

DISTROLISTS

PERSONS			PLACES				THINGS		
INFLUENCERS	AUTHORS	PROFESSIONALS	BLOGS	MICRO BLOGS	PODCASTS	YOUTUBE	APPS	BOOKS	PRODUCTS

These are your DistroLists. If you did your homework from earlier in the book, you already have them. Does each one have 100 items? If not, add more now. If you didn't start your DistroLists earlier, start creating them on a notepad, in a Word document, spreadsheet, or wherever! Just start making lists.

In my opinion, the easiest places to start looking for DistroAgents are influencers in the form of social media personalities, blogs, and micro-blog pages like you'll find on Facebook, Instagram, Threads, TikTok, X, etc. Then you have podcasts, YouTube Channels, and businesses.

The first 20 or so are easy, but you really need to dig after that. Initially, I started building a list with 50 names in each category, but as I searched, finding names was harder and harder. Additionally, you don't want to hang your hopes on the first few you find because, in all likelihood, your competitors are probably already working with them. Your goal should be at least 50, ideally 100 for each category.

Most people understand the value of this strategy pretty quickly. It's simple. Here it is again for good measure. Figure out who your ideal customer is, find out who already has their attention, and collaborate with these people to sell your stuff. Once it's explained, it's hard to see selling as much of a challenge anymore, right?

But for some reason, maybe because it is actually so simple, people tend to avoid doing it. Or if they do attempt it, they usually give up too soon and only come up with a handful of results.

To make things easier, I will walk you through a discovery sequence to help you build a huge DistroList! These are my tried and tested ways of searching all categories and types of distribution channel partners with my target buyers' attention. They are grassroot strategies with a few guerilla tactics and hacks mixed in. I've used them for years now, yet they are evergreen and have never failed me. I know without a shadow of a doubt that they will work for you, too.

Please remember that only some of these techniques allow you to search based on really narrow demographics, social traits, or behavioral data. Some give you much broader or narrower results than others. Some may seem simple or obvious, but others require more time investment and commitment. Take the time to work through them all and build out your DistroLists – from product creation and free advertising to paid advertising, building strategic relationships, and full-blown joint ventures. Almost everything from this point forward will center around this list. Follow these steps. Complete one, and add the results to your DistroList. Go straight to the next. It will stack up fast. Do the work. You won't regret it!

Pro Tip

This step is long and detailed, but don't rush through it. Take your time and absorb the information. This is what I did to succeed, and I know it can help you as well.

Discovery Sequence

AI

Let me get this one out of the way first. At the time of this writing, it's brand new. It's new and not something I used when I first started out or during the bulk of my career so far. But it's really made things easier, and today, I'm having a lot of success with it. ChatGPT and Google's Gemini are AI language models that bring immense value to this process. They're like having a virtual assistant who can understand your ideal customer in detail. By simply telling ChatGPT about your target audience, it can generate an extensive list of the places these people frequent, both online and offline. It can also literally identify the things they use before, during, and after using your product. Remember, this space is moving lightning fast, so it's hard to provide guidance at this stage.

A simple example of a prompt could be the following sentence which you'd paste into ChatGPT:

> *I'm looking to expand my business and find the perfect distribution partners. My ideal customers are young professionals interested in fitness and wellness. Can you help me generate a list of online platforms, physical locations, relevant events, products they buy, and influencers they follow? Please make me a list and group them by category.*

Give it a try now. You can make your first list of categories using this approach. Plus, it has a powerful compound effect on every other strategy mentioned in this section. Copy that prompt into ChatGPT to see what I mean.

Google Search

You will get lots of results by simply listing search terms relevant to what you're looking for. A systematic approach to this search is to write out all the phrases you believe people are actively searching for and list everywhere you think your ideal customers might be gathering.

For example, if my target audience is real estate investors, I need to find distribution channels centered around real estate investing.

Phrase	+	Location
Real estate investing	+	Blog
		Podcast
		Influencers
		Thought Leaders
		Forums
		Groups
		Newsletters
		Books

Take this even further by using a search technique called the Alphabet Hack, AKA ABC Hack. Simply type in your phrase followed by a letter in the alphabet.

Keyword/Phrase	+	A
		B
		C

What happens next is Google gives you a suggested search, such as:

Real estate investing	A...
	Apps
	Advisor
	Articles
	Associations near me

Move to the next letter in the alphabet. If we stick with the same phrase, the letter "B" might give you the following:

Real estate investing   B...
Books
Business plan
Basics
Benefits

Go through the alphabet.

For even more results, think of different keywords and phrases associated with your ideal customers. What are some of the outcomes or solutions they might desire? If you are struggling with this, ask ChatGPT to give you suggestions for outcomes or products as solutions for what real estate investors might be looking for.

When looking for real estate investors, we could try phrases like:

Real estate flipping
Multifamily investing   Location search
1031 exchange investments   +   or
IRA/401K investing   Alphabet search
Retirement planning

Take your time with Google searches. You'll find lots of results quickly, and the deeper you dig, the better your results.

Forums and Social News Sites

Join forum threads, discussions, and Q&As related to your industry, and see who regularly engages in discussions. These are great places to find influencers you can collaborate with. Some forums, message boards, and social news sites even show you how many followers or subscribers a user/contributor might have.

To find these sites, type in your keywords or phrases plus the word "forum" in Google:

| Phrase | + | Forum |
| Real estate investing | + | Forum |

Pro Tip

If the forum or social news site is small and/or really niche, consider approaching the site directly to get access to their entire list!

X (formerly Twitter)

As a research tool, X is a fantastic way to find people or accounts with active feeds with many highly engaged, organic followers. You can set your own feeds for specific hashtags, topics, influencers, and other DistroAgents you already know. Once you've done that, you'll see that whenever something great or important about your market comes up, it will surface in your feeds.

This way, it's easier to monitor your feed and watch for personalities and accounts rising to top tweets. These accounts will have the audience groups who are clearly highly engaged at that exact time. Add these personalities and accounts to your DistroList immediately!

Facebook Groups

Whatever your market, there will be a group for you. There are hundreds of thousands of groups covering all kinds of niches in pretty much any market you can think of. People contribute and engage with these groups daily by asking questions, answering questions, sharing thoughts and ideas, networking, or simply keeping up to date with their community.

Whatever they may be doing is all happening in one place. These groups are set up and managed by the people who run the show and, therefore, have a lot of influence. Whether that person is an influencer or appointed administrator, they are the gatekeeper to the group, establish the group rules, control discussions, and can broadcast to the group. Sometimes, group owners and administrators have collected their members' contact information and can connect and engage with them through different platforms like email and text messages/SMS.

To start, go to Facebook. In the main search bar, type in the keyword or phrase plus the word "groups":

Phrase	+	Groups
Real estate	+	Groups

When you click on any of these groups, you'll find one or more ways to contact the group administrators. Add groups of all sizes relevant to your submarket and ideal buyer groups to your DistroList.

YouTube Channels

Even though its functionality is similar to how social media platforms work, you can search YouTube like a search engine. Here's the thing. With other social platforms, people create content and try to engage their users and build up large subscriber numbers. However, one very important difference (or feature) with YouTube is that all those videos are viewable and searchable forever.

Social media platforms, on the other hand, suffer from post degradation, meaning once you post something to your feed, it starts falling to the bottom of your feed as time passes. So, your post has a very short lifespan and will become much more difficult to find over time.

At the time of this writing, some platforms like TikTok use new algorithms that can keep content up and cycling for longer (provided it's being viewed a lot), but post degradation is inherent since the platforms want their users to keep producing content.

However, with YouTube, things are different. Your videos are saved in your channel's library of viewable content and are searchable like with Google. If you don't already know, YouTube is owned by Google, and it's the second-largest search engine after Google itself.

This means really good videos always appear at the top of search results regardless of how old they are. You can find content from YouTube creators that will be specific to what you search for and show you who has your audience's attention. Your job is to contact and collaborate with creators or YouTube channel owners.

Since YouTube is a Google product, the same search mechanics work here. I recommend the ABC search:

Keyword/Phrase   +   A
                                   B
                                   C

Choose the ones closest to your market, such as the ones that best represent what your audience is watching, and add those channels to your DistroList.

Podcast Apps

Podcasts are great. They are usually long format, sometimes 2 hours or more, and you can listen to them whenever you want. I regularly listen to podcasts when traveling on a bus, train, or driving. I also listen to them when cooking, jogging, and (if I'm keeping it real) as a justifiable way to procrastinate and fill time while avoiding doing something else.

Listening to anyone for over an hour is a long time to have someone in your ear, especially if you're a regular listener. The podcaster clearly has your attention, and even if you're listening passively, they still have your interest. As a result, they are bound to have some influence over the decisions you make.

Apple podcasts, Google podcasts, Spotify, and most other podcast apps let you search their entire podcast library by interest. Type a keyword into the main search box, and you'll see all the podcasts that relate to whatever you're looking for. The results will also be ranked by which podcasts are most listened to.

The bottom line is that podcasts target niche audience groups and hold their attention for long periods. Wouldn't it be great to have the podcasters themselves discuss, review, or endorse your business or offer? It's a no-brainer, so go to any of these podcast platforms and start adding names to your DistroList now.

App Stores

Apps are usually designed for a very specific purpose and, therefore, have a highly targeted audience. Collaborations with an app can give you fantastic ways to reach out and engage your target buyers. In fact, that's an understatement. Apps usually have a ton of usage data with an infinitely expanding range of options to get offers in front of their users.

You can go from emailing users to pinging their phones like an SMS message prompting them to check out your stuff. But then, depending on how you decide to collaborate, you could embed your offer deeper within the app's user experience.

For example, you could gamify your offer, such as how apps give something to their users to unlock rewards after certain actions. I've seen a fitness app that tracks calories by tracking their user's movement through wearable gadgets and lets them add their daily nutrition intake within the app. The app offered users a challenge to burn a certain number of calories in a week to unlock a reward. Those who completed the challenge received 3 free classes to a third-party fitness program. That was a company outside the app that collaborated with them and positioned their offer within the app. That was pretty cool, and I actually took the challenge and received the class passes, introducing me to a boutique fitness firm in my city.

There are even more options with virtual or augmented reality and metaverse integration. I'm not a tech guy, but the people who build the apps are. They have the know-how, and they have their audience. If their user base fits your target audience and your offer works for them, you could tap into all that app magic and more.

Start by going to the Apple App Store or Google Play and search apps by keyword (like you did before with podcasts), and add them to your DistroList.

Similarweb

Similarweb allows you to explore competitors who are competing for the same online keywords. However, it has a few other tricks that are quite useful. The platform also lets you see the sites that refer the most traffic to a specific website and tells you where that traffic goes after they leave that site. Yes, you read that correctly. You could literally type in the web address of any person, place, or thing on your DistroList and actually see which websites your target audience went through to get there.

Moreover, you can also see where your target audience goes next! This is a great way to find the persons, places, or things that have captured the attention of your target audience group in places you never thought of. As of this writing, they offer a free trial to new users, so give it a try. The results may surprise you.

Pro Tip

Think about it – wherever that target audience originated from and where they go next is very likely an option you can work with. However, its value is limited when it comes to social platforms like YouTube and Facebook due to their closed nature. It won't tell you who is directing the traffic from those social platforms but rather simply state the amount of traffic coming from Facebook, Instagram, X, YouTube, and so on. Nevertheless, since it tracks all traffic coming into and going out of a website, it is great at identifying smaller blogs and specialized websites. Since people are clicking links into and out of websites, Similarweb will also show you how long these traffic sources and destinations, meaning the ads themselves, have been running. This means you can identify consistent traffic sources, i.e., the ads, that clearly have the attention of your ideal target customers.

BuzzSumo

BuzzSumo is a research tool that tells you what content is popular on the web and where it's shared. By searching using a keyword, you'll receive information on what kind of content your audience is consuming. BuzzSumo will return a list of the top content related to the entered keyword and the links to the sites where the content was found.

You may think, "Hey, isn't that what Google does?" But actually, there is a twist. Let's say you searched for "hot yoga." Instead of a bunch of websites that Google thinks match up, you might get specific content like an article or online video. That specific piece of content might be getting a ton of hits online, and you can see all the sites it originates from, like source sites, and also which sites it's being shared on. These sites could be great DistroAgents you could collaborate with.

Another benefit that's also very helpful is that it tells you which major social platforms are worth searching for potential partners. BuzzSumo will show you how many times the content is shared globally and can even rank the results by total shares or social reach. Simply put, this means it can tell you that Instagram is buzzing with more hot-yoga-related content, whereas Facebook and X seem quiet on the topic. At the time of this writing, BuzzSumo has free and paid options. So, head over there and start adding sites to your DistroList.

Semrush

I use Semrush to tell me who the biggest competitors are for the site in terms of the number of keywords they use. The sites competing for those same keywords are essentially looking to attract the same audience groups I'm looking for.

So if you put in the website of one of the DistroAgents you already have, you'll see all the other online sites competing for the same keyword searches on Google. I recommend searching a variety of potentials in your DistroList, mixing in an even number of persons, places, and things you've already found.

Head to the "organic research" search option when you visit the site. Enter a website, and it will give you all the other sites using and competing for the same keywords. Keep it simple, and add these competing sites to your DistroList.

Pro Tip

The site is quite complex, and when you get there, it's very obviously targeted toward advanced users. Some brain-melting options provide you with all sorts of complex data and analytics, which can take you off course. Stay focused.

Discovery Sequence Summary

That's it for the go-to options I personally use to build my own DistroLists. They are the foundations for how I put together huge lists that can give me access to millions of potential buyers and the persons, places, or things that can influence their buying decisions. I hope you see why it's super important that you follow these steps.

Hacks

But wait, there's more! Like with most things, nothing speeds up a complex or time-consuming process faster than the experience of having done it before. Along the way, you learn a few tricks that speed some things up and find shortcuts to others, and then there are the hacks that let you ride on the coattails of someone else's efforts to get you results faster. Because I want you to have every advantage, I won't hold them back. The next section focuses on useful hacks I've learned along the way.

Google Alerts

Let's start with an easy one. After spending all that time coming up with search phrases, keyword searches, and working your way through the alphabet search, the last thing you want to do is to remember all the good ones and conduct the same search routine every day just in case anything new comes up. That's where this hack comes in. Google has a really handy feature called Google Alerts, which lets you set up personalized alerts for the searches you create and how often you want to receive them. This feature has been around since 2003, and I think a lot of people have forgotten it exists.

You can easily set it up to receive emails weekly or even daily if you want. What's essentially happening is Google conducts the search for you automatically and sends an email with content related to the searches you set up. If you check these alerts regularly, you'll notice who regularly produces content aligned with your brand or market niche.

AI

AI language models like ChatGPT, Google Gemini, and Microsoft Bing are just the beginning of a major transformation in how we access information. Despite being relatively new, these models have already made it easy for most people to interact with AI and obtain valuable insights.

When it comes to finding and assessing potential distribution partners, AI's capabilities are amazing. By telling it what your product or service is, it can make very accurate assumptions on who your ideal clients are, understand where they congregate both online and offline, and even perform searches on platforms it can crawl to gather links and contact details. Imagine how powerful this can be for streamlining the partner search process.

In fact, AI has the potential to revolutionize the entire distribution partner discovery journey. With AI at your side, you can identify the most promising partners with precision and even leverage its abilities to automate your outreach. It could literally find and make first contact on your behalf! The possibilities are endless, and at DistroChannels, we are actively working on harnessing the power of AI to enhance distribution partner strategies.

To explore more about the future of distribution channels and our innovative work, check out DistroList.app for more information.

The AI-driven landscape is rapidly evolving, and we're excited to be part of this transformative journey!

Roundups

You've seen roundups like these on the internet already: "10 fitness bloggers you should be following," "The 25 most fashionable influencers in Manhattan," or "This year's top 10 travel bloggers."

Well, these lists are clearly designed for a specific audience as they tend to have a very narrow focus. That makes the person who put the roundup together (the list owner) a potentially very valuable DistroAgent.

I say that because influencers, bloggers, and content creators generally search for roundups like these because a big part of building their own audiences is to find places they can be showcased and promoted. They actually put themselves forward as applicants to be added to a particular roundup or considered for similar roundups.

That means the person who put together the roundup will likely have many candidates that fit that market. On top of that, we can also assume that they did a fair amount of research in putting together the list to begin with. That's a fantastic way to work with the list owner. Go ahead and search roundups that fit your market and add them to your DistroList.

Follow the Follower

People who have become influencers tend to be inspired by other bigger influencers. These bigger influencers – usually your prime candidates – typically have a lot of smaller versions of themselves in their audience. Often, these "mini-me" influencers offer a slightly different, untapped audience of their own. They may even have better engagement rates with their audience, and because they are smaller, they may offer more cost-effective ways to collaborate.

I would rather have 10 mini-me influencers with an average audience size of 10,000 with high engagement rates than 1 prime influencer with 100,000 followers with lower engagement. Also, if 1 mini-me stops collaborating with you, not all is lost because you still have 9 others in play. Whereas if you lose your prime influencer, you'll have zero access to that audience group.

You could even sort them in a separate column in your spreadsheet titled Mini-Me (as I like to) or, more sensibly, Lookalikes. Either way, go ahead and search through the followers of some of the prime content creators and bloggers you've already found and add more names to your DistroList.

Competitors

Influencers who promote your competition are a great resource, too. Search your chosen phrases, market-related hashtags, or topics and interests on your chosen platform, and see who regularly creates content related to your competitors.

If these influencers are willing to create and share content relevant to your market and are already working with brands similar to yours, they may also be open to working with you. In this case, the benefit to you is that your competitors have tested the water with those influencers. And if they are working with several competitors, then their audience may be a good fit.

Some influencers work exclusively for one brand or under a non-compete agreement for a set time, but they are the minority in the content creation, social media, and blogger world.

So, start snooping on who's promoting your competitor's stuff and add their names to your DistroList.

Affiliate Leaderboards

This hack complements the previous competitor hack and takes it a step further. When looking at your competitors, pay particular attention to the ones who also use affiliates (or influencers as affiliates) to promote their stuff. As before, they've done the leg work for you and have already found, organized, and engaged the same people you want promoting your brand.

The hack here is to join your competitor's affiliate team. Once you're in, there will usually be a leaderboard that, from your point of view, is your competitor showcasing their best affiliates in ranked order of who's selling the most. It's like hitting the jackpot. It's such an easy hack.

All you need to do is find your competitors with affiliate programs. Those who do will usually openly advertise their partnership options on their website – look toward the bottom footer of a website where there is usually an index of all the pages on the site. If they have an affiliate or partnership program, they will likely have links like "affiliate area," "partner portal," or something similar. When you find a business that does, sign up for their program.

As definitions go, this is definitely a hack, but nothing legally restricts you from doing it. I'm not in the business of playing fair. If you aren't breaking any laws, I say go for it. This hack is a great way to get a list of potential partners with a proven track record selling similar stuff and are clearly good at it.

Start making your list, and while you're at it, think about the most competitive compensation plan you can offer them. Figure out how you can pay them way more than they are being paid right now. The honor is in the dollar, as they say, and frankly, you don't have many angles here. It's helpful to remind yourself again that you need them more than they need you!

Books

Searching for books in your market is probably one of the easiest shortcuts. Go over to Amazon right now, or any bookstore for that matter, and type in any keyword or phrase relevant to your market plus the word "book," and you'll probably get a ton of results.

People write books, and those people are experts and thought leaders in their markets. They are an authority on their subject matter. So, if that subject matter is in line with your niche offer, then you now have a potential partner with a very engaged audience.

Bear in mind that it's not just the readers who bought the book who are valuable. Think about all the extra mediums and platforms authors regularly engage with to promote their books. Many of them do speaking engagements with live audiences and have blogs with a lot of subscribers. Some may even have their own podcasts and every other platform that helps them build up their reader base. The point is that they have a lot of reach and are easy to find.

Popular Products

This is similar to the rationale behind searching for books in your market.

There are 2 ways to look for products:

1. Look for popular products that your target audience is buying as solutions to the problems they are having within your market space.
2. Look for the products people are using before, during, and after the one you're looking to promote.

This opens up two paths for building your list. One path gets you a list of popular products that clearly sell well to your target audience. The other path leads you to the people or sites that review those products, which can lead you to another large pool of interested, hot buyers. It's like hitting two birds with one stone. It's a fantastic hack for tapping into some less obvious persons, places, and things that have gathered your ideal audience.

The process is 2 easy-to-follow steps:

1. Search for products relevant to your market and make a list. By itself, this is a great list of potential partners.
2. Start a separate search for reviews for each of those products and list all the people and places reviewing products in your market. Clearly, if the reviewers get a lot of hits, they will be influencing the buying decisions of the audience group you want.

Referrals

Okay, I already know what you're thinking, and I kind of agree with you. Referrals seem a little obvious, right? But I'm keeping it here as a hack because despite how simple or well-known it is, in my experience, not enough people actually ask. And then, when I tell them to do it, they get results faster than most other tricks of the trade.

If you are already working with a DistroAgent or negotiating with them, the easiest hack is simply asking them for referrals. They will almost definitely be able to refer you to other influencers, affiliates, or businesses within their market. This strategy works in every sales environment, and it's no different here. The fact is that the people who are already working with you tend to be more helpful than not. You can improve your chances further (and I always do this) by offering an incentive like a referral fee.

Being referred, or better still, being directly introduced to someone, can really give you a boost. The way I ask for referrals is equally as simple. I literally ask whoever I'm talking with to think of 3 referrals that would be a good fit. I learned this psychological tactic in my days as a headhunter – ask people for a specific number of referrals. Somehow it always works, and you'll be surprised how much people are willing to help.

Q&A Sites

This hack, much like how you ask for referrals, falls under the umbrella of tapping into the good nature of other people. Sites like Quora, Reddit, Discord, Hacker News, Substack, and other equivalents are great places to look for questions people ask about your market. Generally, these Q&A sites are a great research tool, but I call this a hack because it's a shortcut, and most people take it for granted.

I once typed out a question asking for help creating a list of real estate investment companies in Turkey that spoke English. That was it. Within a few hours, someone answered, giving me a list of around 20 websites that I would never have found myself (because I don't speak Turkish and couldn't search effectively). Plus, there were a lot of other helpful responses that assisted me, too. It wasn't a lucky fluke either because I've used Q&A sites for searches like that a lot over the years. If I don't receive a comprehensive list, I'm usually given great advice on how to get it another way. Try it. As the saying goes, "If you don't ask, you don't get."

Let's Do the Math

Create the biggest DistroList you can because it will be the foundation for all your success going forward. I spent days, weeks, and months creating my DistroList. I'd cycle through all these search techniques and hacks and, slowly but surely, build up a huge list. Not everyone on that list will be willing to work with you, so you must give yourself enough options to work with. You really need to commit to this task and persist to create a powerful DistroList.

Have a goal of 1,000+ DistroAgents to share your message. They should be a mix of social media influencers, thought leaders, professionals, and businesses, all with highly targeted audiences. Imagine the impact that would make on your life.

To this day, I create DistroLists for all my wacky ideas. And I believe I'll forever do so. Knowing my ideal customers and finding out who has already gathered them and has the influence to sway their decisions breathes life into almost any idea I drum up.

When I ran my consultancy firm, Core Agents, I had 1,257 DistroAgents engaged and promoting products for me. When I leveraged the trust and faith the audience had in those key influencers, I could trigger a huge volume of sales almost instantly, flooding my sales funnels with new, paying clients. My biggest problem was supply.

> ### Pro Tip
>
> This is a good time to remind you to never, ever, EVER get sloppy with what you're supplying your partners. They will sell whatever it is fast, and that's the point. The due diligence applies to whether you created the product or collaborated with another brand and sold their stuff. Make sure it's legal and does what it says it does. Don't take anyone's word for it. Find out for yourself. Ignorance won't save you, and I can tell you first-hand prison sucks.

Despite my efforts to convince people of the power of this list, too few people take the time to do it. Don't make that mistake. At the end of the day, it's just math, and math doesn't lie! So, let's math the shit out of this. Let's say you created a DistroList and found 50 influencers. Those influencers are a combination of social media personalities, bloggers, podcasters, and small-to-medium businesses with good-sized client lists and great audience demographics that match your ideal buyers.

Let's also say that each influencer averages 25,000 followers, subscribers, readers, or clients. That puts your total audience potential at 1,250,000.

You put together a simple sales page for the thing you're selling and plan for all those influencers to relay your sales message as a recommendation to their respective audiences on the following Thursday at 7 pm.

When the promotion takes place, we assume a few things will happen:

- Only a portion of that audience will actually see the published content – let's assume only 30%, which means 375,000 people noticed it.

- Most who saw the content either won't care or will automatically tune out the message because they realized it was a promotion – let's assume only 30% stopped scrolling, meaning 112,500 people cared.

- Let's be even more realistic and say that most people were busy and decided not to read, listen, or watch the entire message and forgot about it – so again, let's assume only 30% consumed the content, meaning 33,750 people watched it.

- Then only 20% of those remaining people thought the message was relevant to them at that moment and clicked on the link to the sales page – that brings us to 6,750 people landing on your sales page.

- Now, of those who clicked the link, let's say only 20% made a purchase – that's 1,350 sales.

Your total audience potential was 1,250,000, so 1,350 purchases represents just 0.108% of the total audience.

If your thing was priced at $97, you would have just made $130,950 on a Thursday evening at around 7 pm-ish on the back of an endorsement from just 50 influencers with about 25,000 followers each. That's not a super-high follower number if you didn't already know.

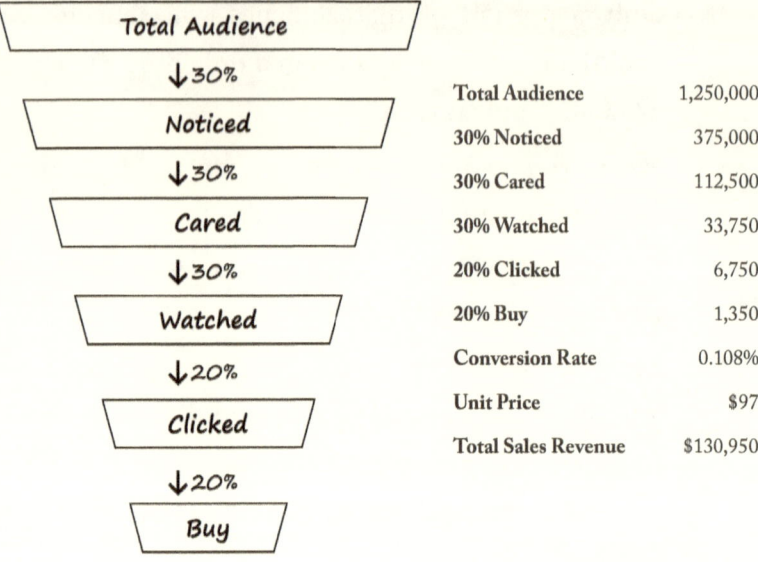

Total Audience	1,250,000
30% Noticed	375,000
30% Cared	112,500
30% Watched	33,750
20% Clicked	6,750
20% Buy	1,350
Conversion Rate	0.108%
Unit Price	$97
Total Sales Revenue	$130,950

Even if you paid the influencers 30% of the sales price as a commission, you still made a gross profit of $91,665 before other expenses. And if your cost per unit sold (as expenses) was an additional 30%, meaning your profit before taxes is only 40% of the total, you made $52,380 that Thursday evening.

A More Conservative Estimate

Want to make that even more conservative? Let's say that 20% didn't actually purchase your product. Let's just say they just considered your product, and only 20% of those people actually followed through and bought the product. That would take us down to 270 paying customers. At $97, you would still make a cool $26,190. Not too shabby!

Continuing with the math… You pay the influencers 30% of the sales price as a commission, which would result in a gross profit of $18,333 before other expenses. And if your cost per unit sold (as expenses) was an additional 30%, meaning your profit before taxes is only 40% of the total, you made $7,333 that Thursday evening.

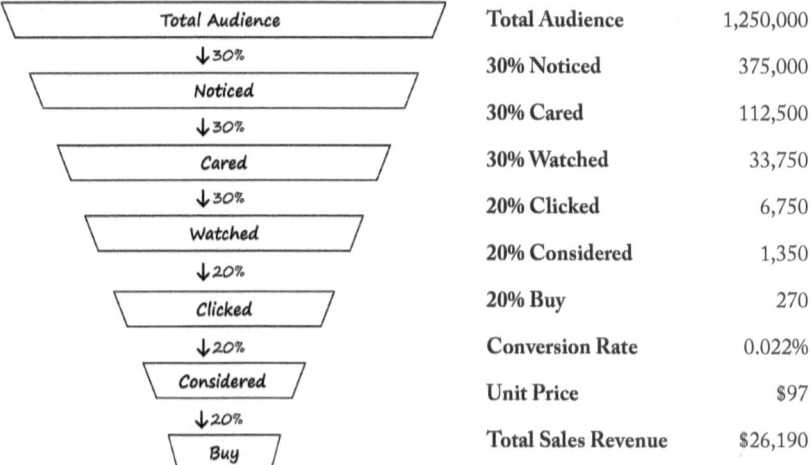

Total Audience	1,250,000
30% Noticed	375,000
30% Cared	112,500
30% Watched	33,750
20% Clicked	6,750
20% Considered	1,350
20% Buy	270
Conversion Rate	0.022%
Unit Price	$97
Total Sales Revenue	$26,190

Just Imagine

With either calculation, imagine if you had 1,257 DistroAgents with 25,000 followers each instead of 50. What if they had more than 25,000 followers each? What if you sold something priced higher than $97? What if you promoted every week that month and even multiple times a week... get the picture?

Pro Tip

By the way, you can have a ton of fun with these numbers! To make the math easy, we created a Potential Sales Calculator that you can access for free at DistroList.app. Go ahead and check it out to see what you could be making.

The Recipe

So, what do you do next? The answer is easy, isn't it? All you need to do is contact every person, place, and thing on your DistroList and convince them to work for you. After that, naturally, they'll start selling your stuff, and then you can take it easy and watch the money roll in while you spend a little bit of time here and there meeting them, building rapport with them, and generally steering them in the direction you want them to take.

Well, not exactly. On the one hand, it is actually that simple. But on the other hand, like when doing most things for the first time, it's a task much easier said than done, especially closing a deal. Think back to your life experiences when you had to do things for the first time. What helped you get through it?

When my daughter was 4, my wife took her out for ice cream, and my little girl ordered her own ice cream. Initially, she did not want to do it. But she had seen other children order by themselves, so deep down, she wanted to do it, too, especially since the other kids could be a little cheeky and get extra ice cream by asking to try different flavors and toppings.

But as soon as she was prompted to ask, she became shy and told her mum to order for her. But on that day, she ordered for herself. So, what changed? Well this time, my daughter was told exactly what to say. She was given a script – just like when my father gave me a script for buying gum.

Having a guide, telling her exactly what to say and when to say it, reduced that paralyzing fear of failure. If you think about it, giving someone a script is a very natural thing to do. How many times have you witnessed parents teaching children that way? How were you first taught to order?

Scripts are needed in all stages of our lives, even with things we are already familiar with, such as dating or asking for a raise, where you might be nervous about what to say to open up the conversation.

Have you ever felt more comfortable when a friend has given you a nudge, along with what you should say? You know the one I'm talking about – it's usually introduced with the universal "just say this…" Well, that's a script. They help us move from inaction to action.

Having a script is super important. It's why in every sales environment, a salesperson is always given a script, and lots of do-and-don't guidelines. The reason is that when you first start, you will be crap. But you will get better at it the more you do it. Actually, a script is like having a map through the woods. As long as you follow it, you can navigate through it. And by the time you emerge, you'll have found your voice and your own style. Use these opener scripts to start your journey right away.

Opener Scripts

When making your first approach, be prepared and know how your partnership, brand, or offer can benefit them and their audience. Not doing your research is not smart. You're reading this book because you want to get it right the first go around, right? Okay, then start by looking at their social media pages. Look for content like recent posts, videos, and press releases that you can relate to, and tailor your message around them.

Don't overdo it, though. I don't want you skirting around the real reason for contacting them, so don't be too long-winded or confusing. The trick is to highlight the relevance of the collaboration, what you want out of it, and that it will benefit them. Finally, you want to know where you stand with them quickly, so also ask a question, such as a call to action, with a response time. Make it as simple and easy as possible for the other side to respond with a yes, no, or maybe. So, how do you get all that across in a quick opener statement?

As a social media direct message (DM), you could say something like:

> *Hi! Your [Brand/Page] caught my attention, and I'm genuinely impressed by the content you produce around [Topic/Product]. I'm interested in discussing the possibility of a sponsored campaign together. If you're available this week, I'd appreciate a quick chat. You can contact me at [Contact Information].*

You could make the DM a little longer:

> *Hey there! I couldn't help but notice your [Brand/Page] and the incredible content you create about [Topic/Product]. I must say, I'm really impressed!*
>
> *I'm reaching out because I have this exciting idea. I think there's a fantastic opportunity for us to collaborate on a sponsored campaign.*

If you're available this week, I'd love to hop on a quick call to discuss the details. I'm eager to explore how we can work together to create something amazing!

Feel free to contact me at [Contact Information]. Looking forward to connecting with you!

Or you could write an email like this:

Hi [Prospect's Name],

I hope this email finds you well. I wanted to reach out and discuss a potential collaboration that could greatly benefit both our brands.

I must say, I'm truly impressed by your [Brand/Page], especially the recent post about [Quick Reference]. It's clear that our audiences share similar interests, and I believe there's a valuable opportunity for us to work together in a non-competitive but profitable way.

Would you be open to exploring options like [a Sponsored Campaign/a Joint Venture Promotion/joining our exclusive brand ambassador program]? I have some ideas that I think could yield great results. If you're available, I suggest discussing this further tomorrow at 3 pm EST. However, I'm flexible and can adjust to a time that suits you better.

Looking forward to the possibility of collaborating with you and creating something remarkable.

Best regards,
[Your Name]

A less-formal approach:

Hey [Prospect's Name]!

Hope you're doing great! I wanted to shoot you a quick message because I think there's an exciting opportunity for us to join forces and create something together.

I gotta say, I'm loving your [Brand/Page]! That recent post about [Quick Reference] really caught my eye. It's clear that we share a similar vibe and have audiences that would love what we can bring to the table.

So, here's the deal: I've been thinking about [a Sponsored Campaign/a Joint Venture Promotion/joining our exclusive brand ambassador program]. Our collaboration could be a win-win, serving our audiences in a way that's both awesome and profitable.

How about we hop on a call to discuss some ideas I have? Tomorrow at 3 pm EST would work for me, but if you prefer a different time, just let me know!

Can't wait to chat and explore the possibilities of working together!

Cheers,
[Your Name]

See how short and sweet those examples are? You don't want to write your life story and expect someone to read it all. Focus on being concise and to the point. Notice how I let them know I follow them and that their content and audience demographic are relevant to my brand. I use terms like sponsored post campaign, joint ventures, and brand ambassador, which signals that there is some money to be made by working with me. At the end, I let them know how to get in touch and a suggested time if they are interested.

Here's another example:

> Hi [Prospect's Name]
>
> My name is [Your Name] from [Company]. I've been following your [Brand/Page] and love your content about [Topic/Products].
>
> I wanted to reach out and discuss the possibility of working together. I genuinely believe that my product would be a fantastic fit for your audience.
>
> If you're open to it, I'd love to schedule a phone call this week to chat about a potential collaboration. I'm confident that our partnership could bring immense value to both our audiences.
>
> Looking forward to connecting with you.
>
> Kind regards,
> [Your Name]

You could even make your offer stand out more by making it sound like an exclusive invitation. Start the message with something like:

- "You're being considered for our exclusive partner program,"

- "Join our approved brand ambassador program," or
- "Invite-only, exclusive partner opportunity."

But don't forget to personalize and tailor your message the way you did for the others. If you don't, you risk having your message considered spam.

> *Hi [Prospect's Name],*
>
> *Exciting news! You're being considered for our exclusive partner program.*
>
> *I'm [Your Name] from [Company], and I've been closely following your [Brand/Page] since [Specific Post/Event/Date]. Your [Products/Posts/Audience] perfectly align with our values, and we see great potential for collaboration.*
>
> *I'd love to have a conversation with you to discuss this opportunity further. Are you available for a call this week? How about tomorrow at 4 pm EST? If that doesn't work, please let me know a time that suits you better.*
>
> *I'm looking forward to hearing from you and exploring some options.*
>
> *Best regards,*
> *[Your Name]*

As far as openers go, those templates should be enough to break the barrier and get you started. By the way, don't contact someone on all social media platforms and emails at the same time. That is spammy, rude, and annoying. Most businesses and influencers will specify an email address or have contact instructions related to business partnerships.

If they don't list anything specific, I recommend an email or direct message on the social media account that looks like they are most active on. Try one first and wait a few days before attempting the next. I want you to reach out to as many potential partners as possible without being spammy.

That is your game plan right now. Your job is to reach out to everyone on your DistroList. Drop these templates into DMs, paste them into emails, and read from them if you're calling a company or person directly.

Here's a telephone opener script:

> *You: Hey [Prospect's Name], it's [Your Name] calling from [Company]. How's it going?*
>
> *Prospect: Oh, hey! I'm doing alright, thanks. What's up?*
>
> *You: I just wanted to chat with you because I've been checking out your [Brand/Page], and I gotta say, I'm really impressed by the content you create about [Topic/Product]. You have some great stuff going on.*
>
> *Prospect: Thanks, I appreciate it!*
>
> *You: No problem! So, the reason I'm reaching out is that I've been thinking about a potential collaboration between our*

brands. I believe we could do a sponsored campaign together that would be a win-win for both of us.

Prospect: Hmm, interesting. What are you thinking?

See, not rocket science is it. It's the same opener as with the DMs and emails. My point here is to NOT over complicate things. It's a numbers game where each prospect could drive in countless sales.

The Initial Pitch

Now it's time to get into the good stuff and pitch your offer. And if you're worried about how to pitch your offer, don't because I'm about to share a killer elevator pitch hack that's super easy to use.

Remember, you'll need to adjust the script based on their responses and continue the conversation in a friendly and conversational manner. Feel free to personalize these as you wish and adjust them for whatever medium you use for reaching out.

Like I said, this is a numbers game. Many people will say they are not interested, but it's really important that you stick with the plan. Feeling disheartened, deflated, upset, or generally unmotivated when someone says no is completely normal. It's your job to ignore all that and persevere.

Any number of reasons could be why they chose not to work with you. It doesn't matter how good your product is or how much you are willing to pay. Don't think about what you can do to change their minds because there'll be time for that later. Right now, focus on getting through your entire DistroList. While you accumulate a lot of *no* answers, you'll also be getting a lot of *yes* and *maybe* responses! Why? Because math and the law of averages are a real thing.

While I have no idea what they will specifically say to you when they say yes or maybe, I know where the conversation needs to go and what you need to say. Your job is to reel them in and recruit them. To do that, you need to capture their interest by quickly pitching *why* they should work with you and *how* they will work with you.

This is essentially an elevator pitch. Prepare and practice it so that you can fire it off effectively and with enthusiasm. Don't get too fancy with it – keep it simple. Here's one of the simplest, most tried, and tested elevator script structures ever. You can't go wrong with it. It's dummy-proof. I know because I've used it for years.

It goes like this:

> *You know how [Define Problem]. Well, what we do is [Solve Problem]. Does that make sense?*

Pause and give them a moment to respond. If they don't quite grasp it initially, don't worry. Simply explain it again clearly and concisely. Once they confirm it makes sense, you're ready to move forward.

Continue:

> *Now, here's the exciting part. I'd love to work with you, and here's what I have in mind: [Explain how you intend to collaborate]. If we work together, we can create something amazing and bring value to both our brands.*

For example, you know how when people talk about their ideas, they sometimes get far too complex and can become lost in their own details? If people are confused or cannot see how an idea is relevant, they'll lose interest, right? Well, *this script structure quickly* gets someone on the same page by highlighting a problem they can actually relate to. Doing that opens up the space to explain your solution in a way that's now relevant to them. Does that make sense?

Did you see what I did there? I'm teaching by example... I'm using the structure to sell you on the rationale just like how I want you to use it to sell to your customers: highlight the problem and then offer a solution.

Here's another example. If I contacted you hoping you would promote my DistroList platform, my pitch would go something like this:

> **You know how** *entrepreneurs often struggle to get off the ground because the cost of marketing and hiring a bunch of salespeople can get really expensive really fast.*

Well, we created DistroLists to connect you to all the persons, places, and things that have the attention of your target buyers without the expensive marketing budgets or the hassle of hiring and managing a sales team. That means you can access an army of on-demand sales people who are ready to promote your products or services directly to their own networks, audiences, and contacts.

After that, you'd naturally start discussing how you'd like to collaborate with them going forward:

Now, here's the exciting part. I'd love to work with you, and this is what I have in mind. Since your audience is a perfect match for this opportunity and because you have the influence and authority to promote this product to them, I propose a joint venture promotion. For every person from your audience who subscribes to our platform, you will receive a generous 30% cut of their membership fee for the duration of their entire subscription duration. Imagine if 1,000 people sign up to our minimum membership, which is priced at $100 per month, you would earn $30,000 per month. It's an incredible chance to maximize your earnings while providing real value to your audience. If we work together, we can create something amazing and bring value to both our brands.

When I go through this process, which is all the time, I think of it as inviting people to a party I organized. I don't think of it as recruitment or a job offer – even though that's exactly what it is in reality. My goal is to interest someone by sharing my excitement and enthusiasm for what I'm doing and then explain how they can benefit by joining me.

If you stick to the plan and contact everyone on your DistroList, which should be extensive, to say the least, a ton of people will be ready to promote for you. I'll say it again... the law of averages is real – it's just math. So seriously, if you have less than 100 names on that list, get back at it.

Before we move on, I want to quickly remind you about the importance of defining your ideal buyer. Every person, place, or thing on your DistroList should have been chosen based on whether they have the ideal buyers for your business in their networks, audiences, and contacts.

The one time I did not do this, and foolishly thought that I could sell something through a DistroNetwork I had previously created, it didn't get me anywhere. I was lazy. I'll admit I even tried a second promotion through the same network and had even worse results. I was lazy and stubborn. It just doesn't work that way. **Knowing your ideal buyer is essential.** The offer must fit their wants and needs, and those buyers need to be gathered in the networks, audiences, and contacts of your chosen DistroAgents. There's just no getting around that.

Pro Tip

When selecting partners, make sure they instantly see the appeal of your opportunity for their audience without conflicting with their brand. It should seamlessly fit in with what they're about, complementing their own brand. Once they make that connection, they should be having visions of how much they can make by working with you. It's human nature. And if they're still hesitant, throw in an upfront promotional fee. Let's face it... a little greed can be a powerful motivator and, provided you followed my 3X rule and have great profit margins, you should get a healthy ROI anyway.

Action Plan

Discovery

- Identify your ideal customer and understand their demographics, interests, and preferences.

- Use AI-powered discovery tools for smarter and more efficient search and data collection.

- Google relevant tools, searching for blogs and websites related to your industry or niche.

- Make a list of influencers who align with your target customer on social media platforms like Facebook, Instagram, TikTok, X, and YouTube.

- Explore relevant Facebook Groups and join those where your target audience is active.

- Use YouTube to find channels that cater to your ideal customer.

- Research podcast apps like Apple Podcasts and Google Podcasts to discover podcasts that attract your target audience.

- Search app stores for apps with a highly targeted audience.

- Leverage tools like SimilarWeb, BuzzSumo, and Semrush to identify websites and content that resonate with your target customers.

- Add all these to your DistroList.

Hacks

- Set up Google Alerts to receive personalized email alerts for relevant industry keywords and updates on the latest trends.

- Use AI tools to locate partners and automate your outreach.

- Look for roundup lists in your industry featuring influencers, bloggers, or content creators actively seeking opportunities to be showcased.

- Follow the followers of larger influencers in your industry to find mini-me influencers with engaged audiences.

- Explore influencers promoting your competitors.

- Search Q&A sites like Quora and Reddit to find people seeking recommendations or advice related to your industry.

- Ask your current DistroAgents for referrals and consider offering a referral fee to increase your chances of receiving valuable recommendations.

- Dedicate time and effort to build a powerful DistroList with over 1,000 potential DistroAgents.

Prepare Your Scripts

- Develop opener scripts tailored to different communication channels, such as social media DMs, emails, and phone calls.

- Personalize your messages to express admiration for the potential partner's content or brand and highlight the relevance of the collaboration, being concise and adding a touch of exclusivity to make your offer stand out.

- Practice delivering an elevator pitch that concisely conveys your message and captures attention.

Most Importantly

- Pitch your offer effectively to capture the interest of potential partners.
- Pitch to everyone on your DistroList, accepting that some, perhaps many, will reject you.
- Continue to add to your DistroList.

Step 4: Management and Optimization

This brings us to the final phase of Part 3: Accelerate Growth, Drive Up Sales. If you've followed my recipe, you will have recruited a ton of DistroAgents, and they are going to do exactly what you ask and start promoting, right?

Thankfully, the answer is mostly yes, at least to begin with. Think of yourself as a skilled circus performer, spinning multiple plates on sticks. It's like a juggling act where you have to keep all the plates spinning smoothly. Those plates will keep twirling if you're attentive and on top of things. But if you let them slow down or neglect them, disaster strikes – they wobble, teeter, and come crashing down.

So, here's the deal. Your job is to stay actively involved, supporting and nurturing your DistroAgents. Keep them motivated, provide guidance, and give them the tools they need to succeed. Stay committed and keep the momentum going to ensure their promotional efforts continue to shine. Your DistroAgents are your business' secret weapons. Treat them like the valuable assets they are, and together, you'll achieve remarkable results.

Your job is to split your time between them all and try to ensure they keep promoting for you and performing at their best. To do this properly, you need to consider a few things because very soon after starting, your DistroAgents will fall into three groups.

The first group will start promoting and immediately make money. So predictably, they will want to continue promoting. This group will undoubtedly be your most loved, and naturally, you'll want to keep them happy. Not only do you benefit from the revenue they bring in, but they are also your best ambassadors for making other DistroAgents want more! By demonstrating their success, you'll motivate others to work smarter and harder.

The next group is promoting for you, but they didn't see immediate results or do as well as they expected. There is a higher risk that this group will lose motivation and not continue to promote your stuff. You need to work with them and show them how they can get results. A little nurturing will go a long way and can turn them into great performers. Remember, you picked them because they have networks, audiences, and contacts filled with your ideal buyers. Help yourself by helping them.

The final group contains those who ghosted you. They agreed to promote, but when the time came, for whatever reason, they decided not to promote. But just like with the previous group, they have access and influence over the larger groups you want. So take the time to re-engage with them and try to spur them into action.

Management 101

Here's another little confession… I am a terrible, terrible manager. Just ask anyone who's ever worked for me. I really hate this job. I always try to be nice, and I'm way too lenient and much too forgiving. It's my nature. I can't help it.

And when it comes to the financials, all I care about is my businesses' top-line profits (total revenue before deducting any expenses). My way is to focus on doing what I do best and drive in as many sales as possible so that I never have to worry about expenses. As long as my profits are 10X of my expenses, I could care less about budgeting, expense management, and bookkeeping. There are better people for those jobs, and I know it.

But despite my shortcomings, I managed 1,257 businesses and people who all worked very hard to promote what I wanted. They did it around the world and in 20+ languages. So, how do you do all that in a way that's so easy you could do it blindfolded?

Okay, maybe not literally with a blindfold on, but imagine accomplishing all this while simultaneously handling other critical aspects of your business. Picture yourself running day-to-day operations, working on new product development, managing your existing employees, dealing with investor relations, trying (and failing) to maintain a healthy work-life balance, and struggling with sleep deprivation, poor stress management, excessive alcohol consumption, and flat out substance abuse that push you to the brink of a constant blackout.

Too much? Well, that was me at one point. So clearly, other factors made me a bad manager. But I was successfully managing 1,257 DistroAgents and pulling in $10M in monthly sales. My sales grew every month, and I was inundated with partner requests from DistroAgents, from countries I'd never heard of. My big challenge became finding a product with enough supply to feed the growing demand of my network.

Eventually, if you follow these steps, your DistroNetwork will reach a similar point. It becomes a sales machine that eventually starts to work on autopilot, where you make lots of money, around the clock, in every country, every language, every day. And you can achieve that, regardless of how complex the sales process, without having to do very much work yourself. Seriously, whether it's yoga mats or investment securities, it'll work just the same.

Let's call this the point of reaching DistroUtopia. Why? Because DistroUtopia sounds cool to me, that's why. But more on that in Part 4: Achieve Massive Scale, Worldwide, 24/7 Nonstop. For now, let's focus on the day-to-day operations of working with your DistroAgents.

It sucks that I had to fail so hard to get things right and see the light. Oh, and I must be honest about another point. There's actually a lot of management advice and business development strategies that could find their home in this step. In fact, some of the stuff I learned in business school, business books, from other business people, or what I've picked up over the years of simply being active in business sounds way better than what I'm about to say. It's true, I was tempted to include some of those theories and concepts. But that wouldn't be true to what I actually did. I'd just be doing that to make myself look smarter than I am.

Effective Communication

Like the rest of this book, I want to keep it real and share how I hacked my way through. So, let's get down to business. There are 3 underlying principles you must put into play every day for this to work.

These principles need to be the core of your approach **every single day**:

1. Meet with all your DistroAgents in any way you can.
2. Keep an open line of communication with them.
3. Provide as much support and assistance as humanly possible.

By embracing these principles as your daily ethos, you'll set yourself up for monumental success in building and nurturing your DistroNetwork. No matter what was going on with my business or life, I needed to stick to my principles or risk losing my DistroAgents.

But let's get real… it will become very difficult to meet everyone in person or personally call every DistroAgent who has a question for you. And also, what does support mean in real terms anyway?

When I first started out, I actually met every one of my DistroAgents face-to-face. I'd entertain them, too. I bought them dinner and drinks all the time. It was fun at first, but it gets expensive and is really time-consuming. As other team members started regularly onboarding DistroAgents, meeting them all eventually became unrealistic and unfeasible. There were simply too many of them. Instead, I made sure I personally called them all, preferably a video call when possible. I even grew to use online webinar and video conference software to welcome many DistroAgents simultaneously, too.

Even if you only do this when they first join, it shows your DistroAgents that you value them and they are important to your business. It's like when you go to a party, and the host welcomes you, giving you a quick tour and introductions. Think about that scenario and how you felt with a warm welcome versus none at all.

Remember, you need them more than they need you. I also kept an open line of communication and quickly responded to any questions or queries. In the beginning, doing this yourself is fine, but directly picking up calls, texting, and emailing will have you glued to your phone all day and night.

And when I say all times of the day or night, I'm not simply referring to working with other countries in different time zones. DistroAgents are notoriously lazy and entitled (they know you need them), so they will contact you whenever they have a fleeting thought. It can get bad. Trust me, I know. You'll know what I'm talking about soon enough. Operating like this will fill your time and distract you from other vital areas in your life, both in business and your personal life.

Regarding support, I provided hands-on assistance to promote and even directly help close deals. I quickly became the sales and marketing support and executive assistant to every one of my

DistroAgents. I provided tailor-made brochures, sales funnel web pages, and other marketing collateral to help them. Again, in the beginning, this is fine, and you should definitely help where you can, but as you grow, this will become more difficult for you to do.

Plus, the more you do it, the more they will expect it from you. You know the old saying about spreading too little butter over too much bread? Well, that saying will perfectly resemble your daily output. You won't be able to give any single DistroAgent the attention and time they deserve, meaning whatever you provide them will suffer in quality and usefulness.

So, how do you relieve the pressure? Simple… hire a bunch of people to do all that for you. Sure, that'll work, but here's the thing. You're only just starting out, so hiring a bunch of managers will be expensive and an ongoing cost. Plus, you need to train them, which will spread you even thinner. We are trying to avoid that right now. And we also want to avoid the employee management thing.

This is where technology comes into play. I relied (and still do today) on a few select ways to manage and support my DistroAgents.

Email

Emailing is probably going to be one of the primary modes of contact. You'll tap out emails from your phone, most of the time answering a lot of questions. It gets repetitive. Believe me… I can't tell you how many times I find myself copying and pasting responses I made from one email to another.

As you probably know, you can categorize conversations by email threads and in folders. But the other thing with email is that you can hit up your entire DistroList and active DistroAgents at the same time. Some well-known and easy-to-use email apps like Mailchimp, Constant Contact, and GetResponse exist.

They are all pretty simple to operate initially but can get complex. The easiest thing to do if you don't like fiddling with software is to hire someone to help. It's like fixing your pipes at home. If you can't fix them and don't want to learn, you simply call a plumber. The same applies here, and the good news is that it's easy to find professionals to set up your email campaigns on sites like Upwork, Fiverr, and Freelancer.

Initially, use those email apps to broadcast a single email to your entire list of active DistroAgents. It's perfect for letting them know about new updates, changes, launches, and prizes as rewards for top sellers.

1. Prepare your email   2. Select your Agents   3. Then send when ready

Later, you can set up persistence emails, drip campaigns, or any other sequence or series of emails that are automatically sent at a preset time and date. This is great for hyping up new product launches or even educating your DistroAgents with bitesize content.

You can put whatever content you like in these emails and have them sent automatically, exactly when you want. We can go much deeper down the rabbit hole and get into setting up email sequences that automatically trigger at different stages of a funnel. But honestly, that's overkill at this stage. We'll get into that stuff another time.

SMS and Messaging Apps

Connecting with your DistroAgents quickly and while you're on the move will be crucial for your daily operations. You won't always want or need to write out an email. Perhaps you or your recipient needs a fast response where a thumbs-up emoji may be all that's necessary. This is where SMS and messaging apps come into play, and there are 3 main ways I use them – instant direct communication, creating groups, and SMS and text blasts.

Instant Direct Communication

Quick, informal instant messaging to get in touch and keep your DistroAgents updated is as essential to your day as a knife and fork are to your dinner plate. This fast, effective communication really keeps your DistroAgents informed, engaged, and on board with your mission. I think the informality of instant messaging makes it easier to build stronger bonds and better cultivate and nurture your relationships with your DistroAgents.

You're probably thinking, "Isn't that the same reason I use those messaging apps in my personal life?" And you're right. Feel free to call me Captain Obvious any time. But seriously, I wrote this down to give you permission (because some people need it) to use these non-business-like apps to connect with DistroAgents like you'd use them in your social circles.

In any case, you'll be doing it all day, most days. Plus, that ties directly into my first principle, in that instant messaging will help you close the gap between you and your DistroAgents. You can meet and maintain an open line of communication via instant messaging, sending voice notes and video messages, and making audio and video calls. Most popular messaging apps have features allowing you to do all those things and more.

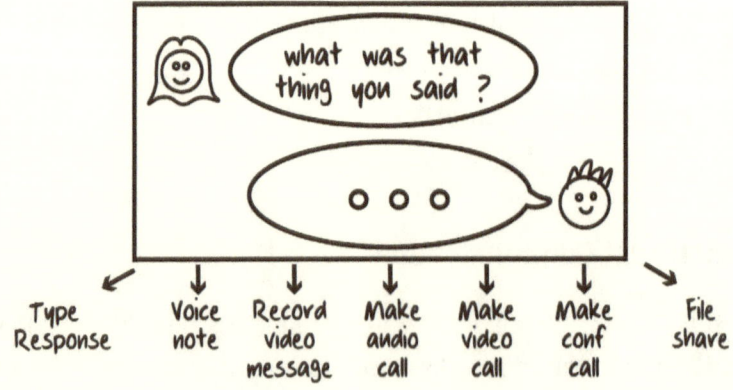

When choosing which messaging apps to use, I'm usually less concerned about the specific features than I am about network adoption. And by that, I mean I prefer to use messaging apps that people are already familiar with. These can be different depending on which country you're in.

For example, when I was working with a lot of DistroAgents in the US, I typically used the iPhone's native iMessenger app along with Facebook Messenger. Why? Because at the time, if I said, "I'll WhatsApp you" or "Join this Telegram group," many of my US DistroAgents had no idea what I was talking about. However, your experience with this may be different because I recently saw a ton of WhatsApp ads on US TV and the internet.

In the UK and my other European neighbors (Britain was still part of the EU back then), WhatsApp was the dominant messenger along with Telegram. Viber was also well-known and widely used, especially in Eastern Europe and the EMEA (Europe, Middle East, and Africa). In China and most other Asian countries, most people used WeChat. As my networks grew and covered more and more countries, I used all those apps interchangeably every day.

Creating Groups

Having a group chat is like calling a quick meeting, with certain groups of people, whenever you want. I'll say what I need to say and observe the feedback. From a remote management standpoint, this is so incredibly valuable.

I use groups all the time in business and my personal life. In the same messenger app, I have groups for my family, close friends, and groups for my business associates. I could have one for my in-house team, one for my top DistroAgents, and another one for all my DistroAgents combined. I rarely found that last one useful, and I'll explain why in a minute. When my DistroAgent is a larger company of people, I usually have a group chat set up for all the key contacts in that company.

Most messenger apps allow you to create groups, with some allowing for more or fewer participants than others. Once you set them up, your DistroAgents will use those group chats every day, at all times, to ask questions and get answers. I'll even bet you'll mute those new message notifications before the end of the first day! Not kidding.

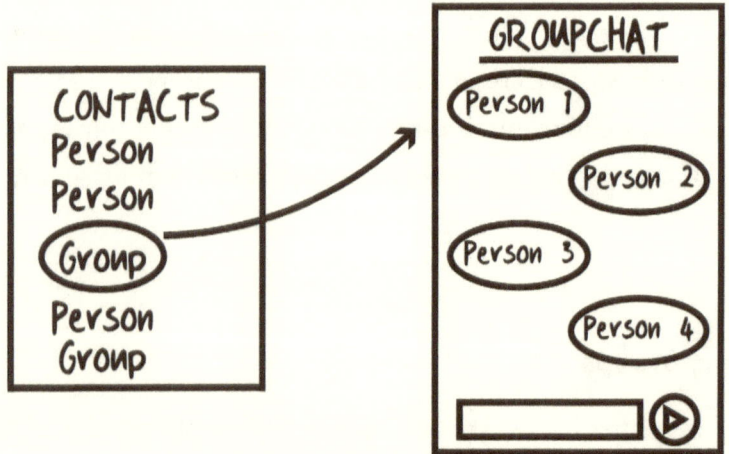

At one point, my main goal was to use groups as a way to get other active DistroAgents to help each other with support inquiries. That didn't turn out so great in practice – DistroAgents are a competitive bunch. Also, when I added all my DistroAgents to one group chat, I saw a lot of blatant poaching and the promotion of other competitors' products. My advice is to compartmentalize to control, divide and conquer, and keep your groups smaller, not larger.

Today, I primarily use groups to convey a tailored message like I would if I were using a one-to-one instant message feature. I can immediately broadcast a message in the form of a simple line of text, a link, or an audio recording, or I could even live stream in some apps and speak to my active participants in real time. It's a great way to instantly generate excitement and start a buzz in your DistroNetwork.

On top of that, I regularly use other really useful practical features. Group chats usually have file-sharing features, meaning I can drop a file from my cell phone or laptop into a group chat and have every one of my active participants download it. I cannot tell you how many times I've done that. I've sent pictures, new logo vectors, newly amended contracts, and a myriad of other things.

SMS and Text Blast

Group chats are great for broadcasting a message and having everyone participating in that group react and interact on the same page.

Text and SMS marketing is about messaging your entire list of DistroAgents individually, simultaneously, so that any response and ensuing dialogue is only between you and that DistroAgent. Sometimes, you need different strokes for different folks, and group chat environments are not the best for that.

I use SMS and text marketing software to send a message to an entire list of cellphone numbers at the same time. I've done this so many times because it works so well. You can literally send a text message to thousands of people instantly. Think about what happens when you actually press send on an SMS/Text program like that. Imagine the hundreds or thousands of cellphones owned by your DistroAgents chiming and vibrating, notifying every one of them that they just received a text from you.

Most people check every single one of their text messages. Would you leave a text message unread? Now, compare that to how you treat your emails. I'll bet there are a lot of emails left unread and unopened in your inbox. In fact, a study conducted by eMarketer in 2022 surveyed over 1,000 businesses that used SMS marketing. The study found that the average open rate for SMS marketing messages is 94%. This is significantly higher than the open rate for email marketing, which is only 20%.

There is SMS and text marketing software that sends messages like a typical text message, and others support more complex messages where you can embed videos, links, GIFs, and more. The email marketing companies I mentioned earlier provide SMS services, too, which is pretty handy because you can manage all your campaigns in one place. No, they have not sponsored me to say this, but they should though!

There are many good options, and for the most part, they are usually very easy to set up. It's typically the same process across all platforms when setting up and sending a campaign.

First, you put in your DistroAgent contacts. You can do this manually or upload them all from a spreadsheet. Next, select the SMS or text marketing function and follow the instructions for preparing your message. Select the contacts you want the message sent to, and set the time and date for the message to fire off.

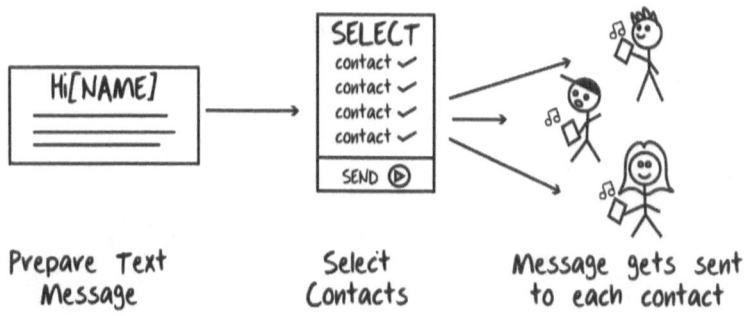

Prepare Text Message	Select Contacts	Message gets sent to each contact

I've used SMS and text marketing software to provide simple notifications like "Check your inbox. We sent you something special." I've even sent a direct link like, "I sent you an email with an important update about _____. Click this link to view it now."

You could even use an SMS/text blast to invite people to a group chat on another App. "Hi [Name], we've just set up an insiders-only group on WeChat. Click this link to take you there now." As you see, I'm pretty much suggesting using SMS/text blasts as a short-form version of an email campaign.

In the same way I use email, I set up entire text message sequences with autoresponders where messages are automatically sent on preset dates and times. Just like with email, I can set things up so that the messages change depending on specific actions the recipient takes or doesn't take.

But I don't want to get ahead of myself. These campaign strategies can get very complex. They are great but are not essential for you to master immediately. I can teach you about that stuff another time. At this stage, all you really need to know is how to communicate a message to all your DistroAgents simultaneously.

Streaming Events

Picture a campfire. If you separate the logs of a campfire, the fire will go out. But if you put them back together again, the fire will light up.

In this analogy, the logs represent people, and the fire represents the positive energy people can generate with each other. If you had one log, you'd have no fire. And therefore, no energy. If you bring two people together, sparks begin to emerge, and you'll start to see some energy. In this case, two logs will give you a flame. Three logs will give you a steady fire. And when you gather four or more, you create a blazing inferno that radiates intense warmth and a ton of energy.

Nothing   Flame   Fire   Blaze

Positive energy is extremely contagious, and I want you to get as many logs together as possible to create a massive blazing fire. And if your logs are your DistroAgents, a wet log would represent a pessimistic or skeptical person.

But guess what happens when you put a wet log into a blazing fire? Well, the wet log will eventually dry out and be on fire, too. The mass of positive energy will generate the excitement and proper motivation you need.

That's why it's crucial to bring all your DistroAgents together at least once per week. And that does not mean you need to spend lots of money on expensive event venues either. What matters is fostering that connection and unleashing the power of positive energy within your network of agents.

Initially, I scheduled live and in-person events like a seminar where I talked to all my DistroAgents. It was expensive but justifiable because it made my DistroAgents feel part of something grand, where everyone fueled one another's fire.

But that quickly became impractical because of limiting factors like audience availability and geography. Not everyone could attend these events when and where I planned them. I tried recording the events for my DistroAgents who couldn't make it, but that was short-lived. I eventually switched to online video conferencing, webinars, and live streaming within my social media platforms. My DistroAgents could watch me present to them live, participate in the discussions, and watch or replay the event at their convenience.

You can use these streaming events for so many reasons. They are great for doing live Q&A sessions and interviews with DistroAgents sharing their success stories, and I've had a lot of success using them to provide full-on training and coaching. I've also regularly used these platforms to sell an offer directly to audiences my DistroAgents invited to the event.

This is not to take anything away from live and in-person presentations. I prefer in-person events because I'm more comfortable in front of real people where I can feel the vibe of a room. But my goal here is to guide you on what to do with a low-cost or no-cost budget so that you minimize your own financial exposure and focus solely on driving as many sales through your DistroNetwork as you can. I need you to stumble your way through my recipe without encountering a financially crippling loss. I want you to read this plan and give it a go yourself. If you don't hit the mark, simply try it again.

For that reason, presenting live over a streaming platform is by far one of the most valuable tools in your kit for engaging your network of DistroAgents. You can do only so much to convey excitement and instill a sense of urgency with emails and messages. The tone of your text may be off. It could be misinterpreted, or perhaps the flurry of emails you sent could be dismissed as spam.

I think I've made my point. Regularly host an online event on your chosen streaming platform to engage your entire DistroNetwork. But if you are anything like me, that's easier said than done.

To be absolutely honest with you, I'm a pretty crappy presenter. I'm even worse when it's just me facing a camera. I constantly mess up what I'm trying to say, and even if I'm alone, I still break out into a cold and nervous sweat. It's just so easy for me to get lost in my words and end up rambling. It's like stage fright takes over, and I end up looking like a clueless fool pretending to be an expert in something I have no business talking about, even though I know it inside out and upside down! It's true. If you see some of my earlier stuff or listen to old interviews of mine, you'll instantly see what I mean.

I know I'm not alone in this, and you may be in the same boat as me when presenting. It's probably safe to say that most people suck at presenting. And for many, being invited to speak in front of a large audience is as welcome as an invitation to swim in a pool filled with flesh-eating piranhas.

Even if you're not shy and happy to talk to lots of people, presenting efficiently and effectively is still difficult. It takes practice. It's an art form. There are special clubs for aspiring presenters, such as the National Speakers Association and Toastmasters. And that is still just the tip of the iceberg. Selling to large audiences takes this art form further.

A simple online search for something like "how to present better" will return a monumental number of books, training programs, courses, and coaches, who can teach you how to present and sell better to large audiences.

But like I said, it's an art form and will take a while for you to become good at it. So like with all the other concepts in this book, I'll give you a shortcut to take the pressure off.

This solution is so simple, but it makes all the difference. All you need to do is team up with others to help you host the event – tada! That's it. Kind of obvious, right? But not really. Most people think they must do this alone because that's what they've seen others do.

Hosting with someone else really helps with the nerves, it gives you someone to banter with, and you can help each other stick to your talking points throughout the session. Plus, having someone else on your side gives you more social proof and further validates what you say.

Think about it from your audience's view. Have you ever noticed how much more you take in from a conversation when you are listening in on it rather than having it directed toward you?

In this case, my audience is my network of DistroAgents. I might want all my DistroAgents to understand something super specific, but they may not hear what I'm saying if I'm talking to them directly. So instead of doing it solo, think about how it might work if I had a few DistroAgents host with me. We could discuss something as a group, knowing that the rest of the DistroAgent network is watching and listening in. We could have a much more organic conversation while projecting a lot of positive energy, just like how news anchors, podcasters, talk show hosts, and award show hosts do it.

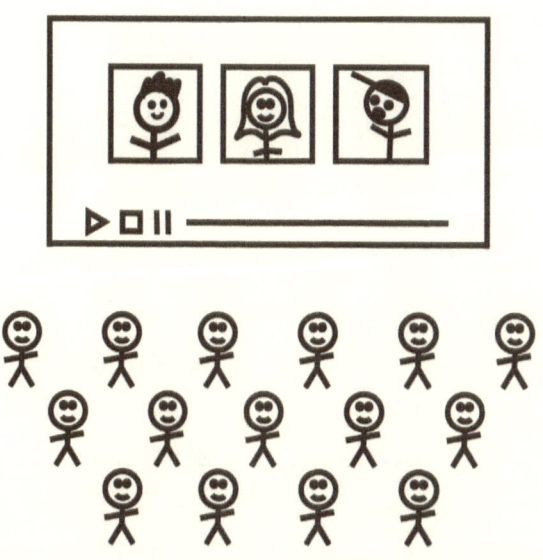

Despite how many people are watching, they are each experiencing your event individually, one person at a time. Going back to my campfire analogy… on the one hand, you need as many DistroAgents as possible to watch the event, but it's equally important to ensure you have enough DistroAgents hosting along with you, too. That way, you can create a blazing hot fire of positive energy. It's amazing how people get more out of conversations when they listen in rather than if someone speaks to them directly.

Pro Tip

Don't host your event with someone negative or skeptical, the wet log. Even with two other positive hosts, there are too few to get a good fire going. Until you are more experienced, your wet logs should only exist in your audience. Your side of the camera should be positive vibes only.

Go ahead and speak to some of the DistroAgents you have a good rapport with, and now let's look at how to set up and schedule your event.

Online Event Setup

Online presentations and webinars give you instant local and global coverage while being the most cost-effective and easiest way to communicate with your entire network. People are already accustomed to watching live-stream content on social platforms like Facebook Live, Instagram Live, and YouTube Live streams. There is virtually no learning curve, and you don't need any fancy studio lighting or recording equipment to get started. The same is true for other platforms that are well-known and widely used in the workplace, such as Zoom, Slack, Microsoft Teams, and other video conferencing software.

I've personally used specialized platforms like GoToMeeting for teleconferences and GoToWebinar for webinars. I had a lot of success using WebinarJam and even the built-in webinar function inside GetResponse. They all do what they advertise, and they do it well. However, if presentation slides, built-in file share, and checkout features are not important to you, you won't need specialized presentation and conference platforms like these. In that case, social media live stream functions will serve you well enough.

Once you choose your co-hosts and the platform, it's time to schedule an online event by sending out invitations to your DistroNetwork.

I plan my online events to be exciting and consistent. Just like how you know exactly when your favorite weekly show is available to watch, I want my DistroAgents to be excited about the event and know exactly when they should tune in. The job here is to set dates and then use your other contact methods to give your DistroAgents a reason to want to watch and engage.

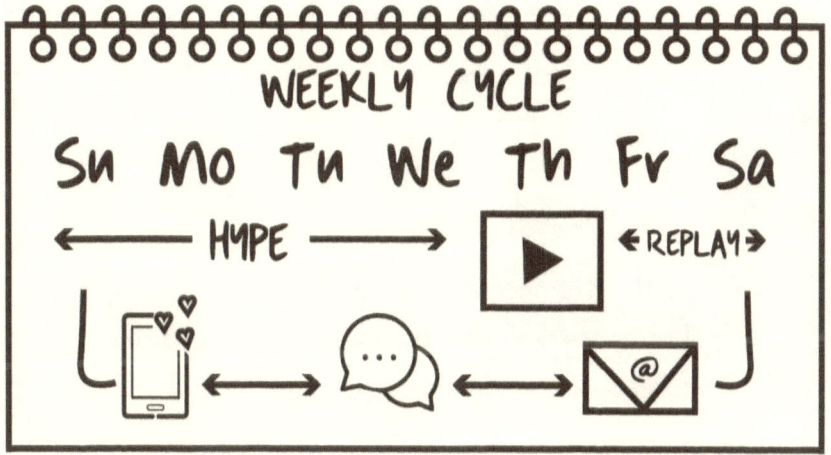

This is an example of how I would schedule my weekly online event. If I decided to set a video conference for Thursdays, I would use the available days before it to hype it up and a few days after to promote the replay for those unable to watch it live.

There's a saying in the advertising world – people will watch anything if it is sufficiently hyped. It's true here, too. Use your messaging apps, group chats, text messaging, and email campaign software to drive as many DistroAgents to watch your event.

Social media is buzzing with successful business personalities who really know how to keep their network and audience engaged. They take things to the next level with all sorts of online events that go beyond the usual private conferences. It's like they created their own reality TV shows that revolve around their business and market. Some of these are like game shows, with awesome prizes to keep everyone excited. And they don't stop there! They also host talk shows where they dive into fascinating topics with cool co-hosts and special guests. You can catch these shows live on platforms like YouTube or listen to them as podcasts on Apple Podcast, Google Podcasts, and Spotify. To top it off, they share their daily lives through vlogs, allowing viewers to connect with them more personally. You feel like you're part of their world. It's a brilliant way to create that personal connection with their audience.

But here's the thing. I personally never did any of that when I was coming up. I think it's definitely the way to go, but you absolutely do NOT need to start off like that to drive home the millions you want.

At this time in your business life cycle, I don't want you to make many different online events for people to engage with. Right now, it's just too time-consuming. I can only teach you what I know to be true. Keep it laser-focused. One weekly pep talk with some teaching and coaching elements will do just fine. Once your DistroAgents drive home a regular, predictable, and profitable amount of sales, you can start doing more. All we are trying to achieve right now is for you to keep your DistroAgents actively engaged, up-to-date, and excited about working with you.

In Part 3, you learned how to accelerate growth and boost sales. We're now set to dive into the final section, Part 4: Achieve Massive Scale, Worldwide, 24/7 Nonstop.

You're about to discover a series of steps that will cover a monumental expansion of your business, which could cover the globe, and how to incorporate a self-regulating, seamlessly automated money-making machine. Get ready to unlock a whole new level of potential.

Action Plan

Action Steps for Management and Optimization of
DistroAgents

- **Stay actively involved with DistroAgents**
  - Continuously support, motivate, and provide tools for
    your DistroAgents.
  - Be attentive to keep them effectively promoting your
    business.
- **Categorize DistroAgents into groups**
  - Group 1: Successful promoters who need
    encouragement to continue.
  - Group 2: Struggling promoters who require guidance
    and nurturing.
  - Group 3: Non-active promoters who need
    re-engagement.
- **Adopt effective communication strategies**
  - Maintain regular contact with all DistroAgents.
  - Keep communication lines open and provide
    substantial support.
- **Use email for broad communication**
  - Use email platforms like Mailchimp for mass
    communication to update, motivate, and inform
    DistroAgents about new opportunities.
- **Implement SMS and messaging apps**
  - Use instant messaging for direct and quick
    communication.
  - Create group chats for efficient communication with
    different segments of DistroAgents.

- Employ SMS/text blasts for individual, simultaneous messaging.

- **Host streaming events**

  - Regularly conduct online events like webinars or live streams to engage with DistroAgents, provide training, and maintain their enthusiasm.

- **Team up for online events**

  - Collaborate with co-hosts to alleviate presentation pressures and enhance engagement during online events.

- **Optimize online event setup**

  - Choose a suitable platform, such as Zoom or Facebook Live, for your online events.
  - Schedule events consistently, and use multiple communication channels to hype them up.
  - Focus on a single regular event to maintain focus and manage time effectively.

Part 4

ACHIEVE MASSIVE SCALE, WORLDWIDE, 24/7 NONSTOP

"Sell that offer super fast, on autopilot, throughout the world and around the clock"

DistroUtopia

Close your eyes, and imagine an army of DistroAgents promoting your business like crazy. You don't even need to manage them directly, meaning your entire sales process is effectively running on autopilot. You'll grow your business and make money around the clock without worrying about it. How would that change your life? Picture having the time to enjoy all the other stuff you want to do. It took me around 10 years of trial and error to reach DistroUtopia, and I will now share with you the tricks of the trade that actually matter in about 20 more minutes of reading. Give or take.

"DistroUtopia" combines the words "distribution"and "utopia" to symbolize the ideal state of distribution within your business. It represents the concept of achieving a perfect, self-regulating sales system that leads to a utopian level of success. The concepts I've shared within this book are actually the secrets behind a lot of the success you see with companies today, and this book dives into the strategies and insights I have learned that make that happen. This book is your recipe for transforming your business into a total success story. This final part, DistroUtopia, is about maximizing your results so that your business takes you to the success you've dreamed of. Let's pause and take stock of where we are right now.

If you followed my recipe, regardless of how much money you have made, you'll have accomplished major things that will serve as the foundation for your success. You have a great business with a fantastic offer that you know, without a doubt, has a big audience of potential buyers. And in Part 2: Create Irresistible Offers, On Demand, you defined exactly who those early buyers are.

You should have a massive, well-researched DistroList and decided on a competitive way to collaborate with them. You contacted and recruited as many as you could and are heavily focused on getting them (and keeping them) excited and motivated to work with you. You've become really good at using social media platforms, direct email, messaging apps, and live recorded video streams to communicate what you want, when you want it, and how you want it done. By now, I wouldn't be surprised if you had someone dedicated to helping you organize and create all of that with you.

I've given you a lot so far – you pretty much have everything you need to build a really successful business. But I want you to have

amazing results. So, I'll give you a few final secret ingredients to add and take this to the next level.

Step 1: DistroPortal

What I call a DistroPortal is essentially a website that serves as a resource area for your entire DistroNetwork. It is their one-stop-shop, which they can visit anytime to find everything they need to perform at their best.

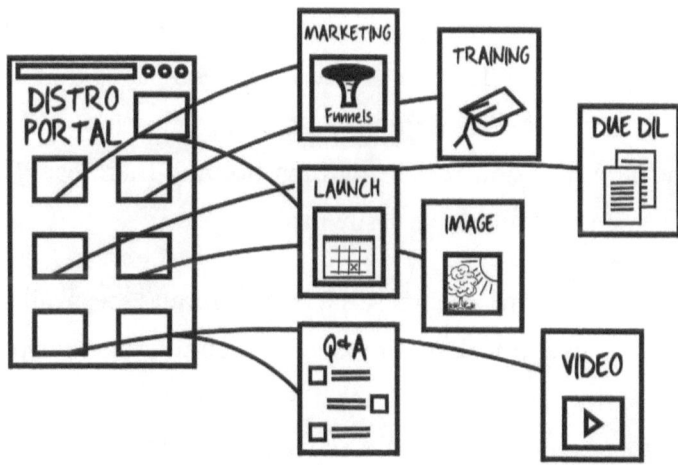

I would have this site behind a login screen to protect any sensitive information I upload, such as marketing collateral, sales material, product information, industry intelligence, and training material. It's also a great place to put a calendar for launch dates and other upcoming events.

I used this space to build a sense of community by adding a forum for questions and answers and leaderboards to instill a sense of competition in my network. So, I don't want people outside my

DistroNetwork poking their noses around. This area is intended to support and empower my DistroAgents with as many on-demand resources as I can muster.

I want you to consider all the things your DistroAgents could possibly need to successfully sell and promote your product. You could have things like downloadable ad copy, which they could use as copy-and-paste templates for their own advertisements. You could even provide word-for-word scripts, images, videos, industry insights, product information, and even sample contracts or other legal stuff if necessary. I've even provided multilingual marketing material and full-blown marketing funnels as a series of web pages that could be downloaded or cloned to be reused. If it can help close a deal, then put it in there. You don't want anything holding them back, least of all a resource you could have easily provided.

All those live-stream events you created should be available for replay in this area. Speaking of videos, depending on your business' complexity, you could even create a series of training videos, such as an online course, as part of a self-paced training and education program. In-depth training like this helps turn your DistroAgents into expert ambassadors for your business. The more they voluntarily learn about your products helps them with their confidence and deepens their commitment to you and your brand.

When building your DistroPortal, I've used drag-and-drop website builders like Squarespace and Wix. It's super easy to build a simple website on these sites, albeit I'm not actually recommending you build one yourself. Unless, of course, you really, really want to.

Speed is everything in this business. Spend a little money and have a professional do it for you. There are plenty of people who make a living putting together really nice sites on these drag-and-drop website builders. There's very little coding involved, if any, so it's very low cost. They can usually put one together in a few hours. It really is that quick. I used them to make some of my DistroPortals.

By the way, I have a plug-and-play option for you as well. Just head over to DistroList.app and sign in or sign up for a free trial. Once you're in, navigate to the marketplace. That's where you can create an offer for your brand and list it. When setting up your offer, you can include various resources like documents, images, videos, and even affiliate links. Yes, that was another shameless plug. Sorry, not sorry.

Step 2: Leaderboards

How do we instill a sense of urgency?

Money alone won't always be enough to motivate everyone. Sure, you will send out as many messages as possible without being spammy and do as many video-streaming events as you can to pep them up and motivate them. You will put as many sales, marketing, and training materials on the DistroPortal as possible. You may think your DistroAgents will perform and promote for you because of how compelling or charismatic you are as a leader. However, you will only become successful if everyone becomes passionate about the brand and mission.

That's true to a degree. As a leader, you have the long-term vision and understand how that vision plays out with every individual in your

DistroNetwork. And for that vision to succeed, you'll probably even be willing to sacrifice your own well-being to fulfill that mission. The truth is… you, as a leader, could spend a lot of time, money, and energy trying to communicate what you want, only to be met with lackluster enthusiasm. Once your DistroAgents leave your video, finish their call with you, or close your email or message in whatever app they were using, regardless of how motivated they were in the moment, they might still do nothing.

It's like when you're scrolling on social media and see something you want to click on, but you keep scrolling on intending to go back and find that link. And then what actually happens is that you forget about it altogether and carry on scrolling. Have you ever done that? I do it all the time.

The same thing happens with your DistroAgents because they are humans, too. They get distracted, lose interest, or get bored. They could be looking at a myriad of other money-making possibilities and bouncing around between them.

I call this a leadership trap, where you spend a lot of time, energy, and money trying to motivate and make them feel good about your brand. But the problem is that you end up with a happy network that never sells anything. Or perhaps more likely, they don't sell anywhere near their potential.

But the opposite can also be true. If you set up a bunch of automated emails and throw in a half-assed conference occasionally, you'll have a network that simply does not care. To get out of this trap, I need to help people help themselves by finding little wins to spur them into action.

Little wins, or at least the feeling of being in a win-state, is an extremely powerful driver. Why... because of decision-making theory, behavioral economics, and because Daniel Kahneman said so, he's really smart and the author of *Thinking, Fast and Slow*. Here's the thing... our brains naturally desire to achieve goals and experience growth to feel progress. That's why we need a little win here and there to feel like we're moving in the right direction. In this case, a win-state is a scenario where one of your DistroAgents conquers a challenge, such as making a sale, and progresses forward. Getting that win will make them feel a sense of accomplishment and motivate them to continue.

So, how do we do that without things getting too complicated?

Well, this is where a little *careful* competition comes into play. I'm talking about a form of gamification to improve productivity and sales and achieve persistent engagement from your DistroAgents. I emphasized being *careful* because I don't want you to get carried away. Competition can be problematic, backfire, and demoralize a network if done badly.

Let me put it another way. Even though competition, in general, creates an adrenaline rush and can add that sense of urgency you're looking for, it can be a very temporary thing. The truth is that most people do not like to be in a constant state of competition.

It's as simple as that. But be careful because even though leaderboards are meant to be motivating and fun, they can do the exact opposite when they are designed badly. For example, if you have 1,000 participants, it's not very motivating to see who the Top 10 are. They are simply too far ahead, and getting to that level might feel unattainable.

The secret behind a good leaderboard is to make your participants feel optimistic about realistically making progress.

When applying leaderboards to my DistroNetworks, I found 2 successful leaderboard dynamics:

1. Position DistroAgents in the middle of the leaderboard so that they only see the people ranked directly above and below them. While seeing how far away you are from the number one spot can be super demotivating, it can be incredibly motivating when you beat the person in front of you.

    Equally, someone just below you, excelling past you, can trigger a strong sense of competition and have you urgently trying to reclaim ground. Have you ever been jogging, and when someone overtakes you, you suddenly have the urge, no matter how tired you are, to speed up and reclaim your position?

2. Another way is to set your leaderboard so that it's constantly refreshing. You could set it so that every week the leaderboard rankings refresh and reset. That way, none of your DistroAgents will fall too far behind. Instead, they will have a renewed sense of hope each week that they can rank higher than the previous week.

These leaderboard dynamics give the participant, our DistroAgent, a renewed sense of hope and urgency to reach a win-state. If achieving that win-state is too challenging because it's too far away, people won't even try.

Think about what might happen if you don't have a leaderboard. After the initial launch, what keeps your DistroAgents pushing hard to promote? Your product or brand is no longer something new to their audiences. With the initial surge of interest over, what keeps them going?

Let's talk about win-states in literal terms. What are they winning? This business is about money and success, after all. Earning a nice title, badge of honor, or sense of personal achievement is good, but let's couple that win-state with something shiny and exciting, too!

I want to tell anyone in my DistroNetwork that they will receive a prize if they hit a target I define in any of my leaderboards. I want them to have something special, which is in addition to the money they'll be making. The prizes themselves can be really great motivators, so it's important to put some thought and money into this.

I have rewarded people with things like bonus cash prizes, luxury watches, cars, and even private jet airtime coupled with all-expenses-paid lavish vacations. They can be anything you want, but it shouldn't be one prize for the biggest DistroAgent.

Reward people for different achievements and tiers. For example, instead of assigning rewards for 1st, 2nd, and 3rd place, you could assign a reward for everyone's first sale. You could have one for those who hit $100 in sales, a larger one for those who hit $10,000, and an even bigger one for $100,000. You get the picture, so think creatively!

You'll see that many of your networks will promote hard for those rewards alone. It might be a little work to set up initially, but creating a dynamic leaderboard with prizes will really take you to the next level.

DistroList.app has a built-in dynamic leaderboard within its affiliate dashboard. The platform tracks the potential of your own DistroNetwork and ranks it against other agents.

Step 3: DistroTeams

I had just started collaborating with a TV and social media personality. I won't share her name for privacy reasons. She had an audience of around 2M, and the bulk of that audience fit the demographics of my ideal buyers. I knew that if she backed my brand and message, she could drive in a lot of sales really, really quickly. I was like a hungry dog, eagerly drooling at a food bowl just out of reach.

But there was a problem. She prided herself on never openly and directly soliciting her audience. She had spent years cultivating and nurturing that audience and building her personal brand. She knew she had the influence to sway her audience toward the thing I wanted them to buy. But she couldn't stomach the risk of being labeled as a sellout.

Being at the top of a leaderboard was not her priority. She wanted to maintain integrity, trust, and goodwill with her audience, which she worked so hard to build.

This is common across many creative people and businesses alike. They focused on creating such a harmonious environment with their audience that the thought of presenting an offer and directly selling to them makes them feel incredibly awkward. Because of that, there would be no use prodding, probing, and pushing them to pepper their audience with my offers.

That might be useful (for me) if I had a very short-term campaign, but it would degrade the value of that DistroAgent and be anti-productive in the long run.

When I realized this, I noticed many more DistroAgents who were similarly positioned. They were all lower down on my leaderboards for overall sales, but that did not mean they were not good. I initially considered them bad performers, but that wasn't the case. In fact, there was an entire host of DistroAgents who were not achieving high sales for various valid reasons. Plenty of other creative personalities and businesses had trouble integrating a sales message elegantly so that it did not tarnish their brand image. There were also fantastic salespeople and marketers who did not have huge audiences to apply their marketing skills to. Some businesses were simply smaller than others, but if they worked together, they might be able to amplify their results without directly bearing the risk of tarnishing their own brand.

This links back to the social proof dynamics I referred to with online video events. By involving more people, you are essentially setting a fire and creating a blaze. Any wet logs will dry out and be set on fire in a blaze.

By pairing some DistroAgents together, I created a team. I approached several of them and asked if they'd be open to teaming up with another person, place, or thing with similar audiences. I was careful to match them based on whether they would complement each other's strengths and ensure no direct conflicts of interest existed.

That was how I formed my first DistroTeam. Honestly, it's become one of my big secrets to getting a DistroNetwork producing quickly! I'm not joking or exaggerating. Teams work.

I usually set it up so that every member of a DistroTeam would link their audiences to one sales page specially created for that DistroTeam. All the profits from sales collected from that page would go into one pot of money, which would be split evenly among the team members.

By setting up this DistroTeam, I realized that team dynamics could be used to motivate my DistroAgents and even shift their behavior without sabotaging their integrity. To be blunt, it meant I could push them into doing what I wanted by relieving them of any direct pressure without being overly pushy or even involved.

That's how I persuaded the TV and social media personality to promote my offer. I presented her with the opportunity to collaborate with another DistroAgent, someone who specializes in working with individuals like her and employs a softer, non-salesy approach to promotions. As a result, she engaged in a co-promotion with this individual who was featured on her podcast, directly connecting with her audience. During the podcast conversation, he seamlessly integrated the promotion, allowing her to authentically endorse the concept in a conversational manner without appearing like a sellout to her audience.

The great thing about getting your DistroAgents to work together cooperatively, as a team, is that it factors in that not everybody is as competitive and needs to sit at the top of a leaderboard. But equally, it also factors in that most people don't want to be the reason why a team falls behind either. As a result, everyone works harder as a team.

So instead of taking the zero-sum approach of only putting time, energy, and money into motivating your best performers, look at all your DistroAgents and consider how to bring their individual strengths together and create a DistroTeam. In the long run, this will generally outperform any of the one-to-one pep talks you might think of.

Step 4: DistroLeaders

I was looking for that big partnership opportunity. At the time, I was selling real estate investment properties. I felt that I knew what the UK buyers' appetite was for these investments and who already had their attention and trust.

By then, I had been building up a network of DistroAgents for some years, so I knew I could sell any of those real estate products very quickly, and I did. I made a lot of money doing so.

It didn't matter that it was real estate either... it could have been anything. I was successful because I took the time to cultivate and nurture a network of distribution channels that gave me direct access to the buyer groups I wanted to sell to.

But here's the thing. I felt a few factors were holding me back from taking my business to the next level. The companies I partnered with were all smaller property developers and could never provide enough supply to satisfy the demand my DistroNetwork generated.

Those developers had properties with 20 to 50 available units. It was far too few and sporadic. I'd sell out one and then wait for the green light to sell to the next. And finding the next project was a task in itself. I was relying on them to supply the demand from the network I cultivated.

Remember Part 1: Empower Yourself, Earn Instantly? The first step was to find the project. In this case, my job was to find the property developer with the real estate project I wanted to sell. The next step was to negotiate my fee, aiming for exclusivity, although I didn't always get it. Next, I found out where my ideal buyers were and recruited whoever already had their attention into my DistroNetwork. Then my job was to mobilize my DistroAgents while training them on the nuances and finer points of this new opportunity.

Much bigger property developers were out there who could give me the larger unit numbers I needed to sell. That would allow me to build sales momentum and raise my brand's X factor since these bigger companies were well-known names with long-established track records. Plus, I'd be selling one thing for longer, helping with my brand identity.

The trouble was finding an opportunity to partner with them. They had a close-knit group of trusted partners they'd relied on year in and year out. I was the underdog, trying to find my way in.

> **Pro Tip**
>
> While this is a great way to get started, depending on which business type you collaborate with, you might find bottlenecks and supply chain issues that don't allow you to scale in line with your DistroNetwork. I'm not saying Part 1 is no longer useful, but there may come a point as your business grows where you will need to upgrade.

One day I received a call from Thomas, VP of sales for a very big developer. He knew me because I knew everyone he knew. That's one of the benefits of building a large network on the back of opportunities I controlled, where I ensured everyone involved received payment. For the most part, that usually ensures you are spoken of in a good light.

What this meant for me was that Thomas was about to open a door I wanted with one of those large property developers. He was offering me a game-changing opportunity. They had thousands of real estate units for me to sell, with many more under development. I wouldn't need to worry about supply at all.

In fact, I'd need to grow the number of DistroAgents in my network to sell faster than their existing partners. I would receive company-level commissions, meaning a level high enough for a company to allocate smaller percentages to its internal sales staff, referral partners, and DistroAgents. In this case, it was a 20% commission on the total value of each sale. I could easily allocate 10%, even 15%, to my DistroAgents on the sales they drive home.

But there was a catch. Thomas said I could not sell these real estate units to buyers in certain territories where they had already established exclusivity agreements with their existing distribution partners. I figured that was fair at first. But then he defined the territories. And my heart sank.

I could not sell in the UK, the US, Australia, or Canada. Practically all of the English-speaking world was off-limits. I thought he was joking, but he wasn't. I knew this opportunity was too good to be true...

Thomas went on to say that I could sell in the rest of the European countries, including Russia, the Middle East, and Asia. He said I could sell in Africa and joked that English is widely spoken in South Africa. So, not all English-speaking countries were off limits. I wasn't laughing. I was immediately deflated. He tried to console me by telling me that I was a great salesman and could do it. My response, littered with foul language, was that I'm a proficient salesperson when selling to an English-speaking buyer. How was I meant to sell in French, German, Spanish, Turkish, Ukrainian, Russian, Arabic, Mandarin, and all the other languages out there?

Even if I had my sales material translated, the ad copy might be all wrong. What might work for the French may be inappropriate for the Germans. I had to also consider the cultural norms. This would normally be a non-issue because I'd be following my recipe for finding those persons, places, and things that have gathered my target audience and asking them to promote for me. But this language barrier would stop me from doing that job properly.

I tried to negotiate my way into being able to sell in the UK, but he said there was nothing he could do. If I wanted to get into the big leagues, I would have to figure out how to make this work.

So, I took the offer. I told myself I'd stick to the plan and set about trying to find my buyer groups in those other countries and contact the persons, places, and things that had gathered them together. The language barrier made it cripplingly slow. It was infuriating, actually. Penetrating the market in a different language felt like a lost cause.

Every day ended the same. I was absolutely exhausted and deflated. I was lucky if I had one meaningful conversation.

I found a few English-speaking people in those countries, but I needed more to have a significant impact. I found some who had the knowledge, experience, and audience that fit my buyer group, but they were few in number. I wasn't going to make the millions I wanted with just a handful of DistroAgents.

I even asked those DistroAgents if they knew anyone else. But they avoided giving me any names because they didn't want to create more competition for themselves. I needed a version of myself in each of those countries. I needed someone who knew the language and cultural norms, and most importantly, I needed them to know the business.

A New Model

I had my moment of clarity – my AHA moment. I needed a person in each of these countries to take over my job. They would need to find, recruit, train, and continuously manage the DistroAgents they onboarded. I needed them to lead their own network of DistroAgents.

That was the only way I could sell what I was offering on a local level, in the correct language, and in a way that met cultural norms and expectations. They needed to understand their territory's unique qualities, characters, economic conditions, and other aspects. They needed to do it in a way I could never achieve by myself.

I needed a two-tiered model like a franchise to create additional versions of myself. I could give full management control to people and businesses locally in those countries. They are the best people to convey my sales message anyway. Why not figure out how to give them more autonomy and further empower them? They are much better positioned to find the buyer groups and effectively contact all the persons, places, and things.

I moved forward with this two-tiered model and created DistroLeaders, whose job was to develop and support their own networks of DistroAgents in their territories. I created 15 DistroLeaders, who created a network of 3,500+ DistroAgents within their regions and neighboring regions they were familiar with.

These DistroLeaders could take on as many DistroAgents as they wanted, and they could even create DistroTeams.

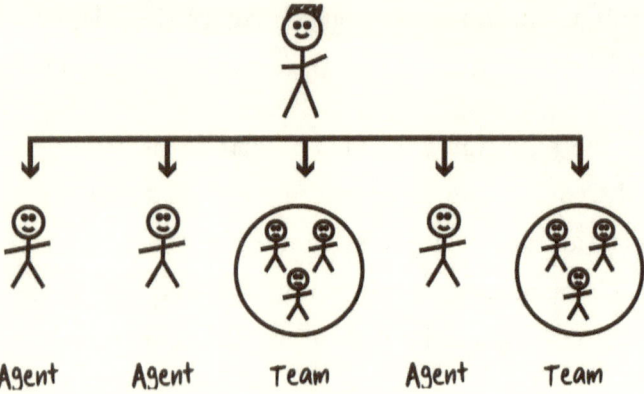

Some people don't like these two-tiered models because it allocates too much money for the DistroLeaders and DistroAgents. It takes money away from what could be retained by the main corporation.

Don't get me wrong because I understand that point of view. But I have also learned that giving up more of my profit to support my long-term vision is worth it. By taking a two-tiered approach, I receive a huge amount of additional brand exposure and a higher overall sales volume. It gives me better control of my business while also giving my end customers a higher-quality experience at a local level. So instead of the direct sales approach and navigating language barriers, I could focus more on my strategy and other key business features.

What would this look like if I tried to achieve these same numbers with a direct sales model? That would mean employing people and salaries. I would need a huge business with thousands of employees and hundreds of department managers, and I would have been highly distracted with managing all that.

Instead, I could do what I do best. With the two-tiered model, I can manage and maintain a huge sales volume with a self-regulating army of 3,000+ sales professionals – all with 1,000+ potential buyers each. And on top of that, I managed all of them with only 6 full-time internal employees.

I also learned I could use this two-tiered approach all the time. It wasn't just useful for penetrating different countries. It's a great way to structure your sales effort.

This is the point I call DistroUtopia, where your entire sales process, your money-making, dream-fulfilling engine runs on autopilot!

You developed a huge distribution network. You identified potential DistroLeaders worldwide who have a deep understanding of their local markets and speak the language. You used your DistroPortal to train, nurture, and equip them with comprehensive knowledge. You encouraged these leaders to form and manage DistroTeams, employing gamification methods like Leaderboards for motivation and network expansion. You implemented a two-tiered model for operational efficiency.

This allows the central organization to concentrate on strategic business aspects, which minimizes your involvement in direct sales. Once this comes together, you have DistroUtopia – a self-sustaining sales system with minimal central oversight, driven by a self-regulating, high-performing sales force.

Action Plan

Action Steps for Achieving DistroUtopia in Your Business

- **Create a DistroPortal**
  - Develop a centralized resource website for DistroAgents.
  - Ensure it includes marketing materials, training resources, sales material, industry intelligence, etc.
  - Implement a login system to keep it exclusive for DistroAgents.

- **Use leaderboards**
  - Introduce leaderboards to create a competitive yet fun environment.
  - Design the leaderboard to motivate by showing DistroAgents close competitors.
  - Regularly refresh rankings to maintain engagement and provide achievable goals.

- **Offer incentives and rewards**
  - Provide incentives and rewards for achieving sales targets.
  - Consider different tiers of rewards to motivate various achievement levels.

- **Form DistroTeams**
  - Pair DistroAgents with complementary skills and audiences.
  - Encourage cooperative teamwork to amplify sales efforts.
  - Create specialized sales pages for DistroTeams for centralized profit sharing.

- **Establish DistroLeaders**
  - Develop a two-tier model by appointing DistroLeaders in different regions.
  - Empower these leaders to manage and support their network of DistroAgents.
  - Allow DistroLeaders autonomy to adapt strategies to local markets and cultures.
- **Focus on strategy and business development**
  - With the two-tier model, concentrate on overall business strategy and growth.
  - Let DistroLeaders handle direct sales and regional management.
- **Use DistroList.app**
  - Leverage DistroList.app for resources, leaderboards, and network management.
  - Use its features to streamline the process of managing your distribution network.

Conclusion

The recipes in *The DistroVerse* are more than just a guide – they are your blueprint to success, driving you toward a future filled with growth, innovation, and sales achievements.

In Part 1: Empower Yourself, Earn Instantly, you discovered the power of strong connections with businesses that value your efforts. You took control of your life and learned how to collaborate with both distribution partners and businesses to make money right away

But you didn't stop there. In Part 2: Create Irresistible Offers, On Demand, you dove deeper into the world of entrepreneurship. You found the market that matched your passions and expertise. Whether you built your own audience from scratch or tapped into existing ones, you learned how to connect with your audience. By understanding their needs and desires, you figured out how to give them exactly what they want. With that knowledge, you created products and services that solidified your place in the market based on their needs.

Your journey continued in Part 3: Accelerate Growth, Drive Up Sales, where you scaled your business and expanded your reach. You positioned your venture as a win-win opportunity and partnered with entities that boosted your credibility. Collaborations, sponsorships, and co-marketing initiatives were your tools to captivate and engage your audience. And most importantly, look at the DistroAgents you assembled. They helped you tap into new sales opportunities for exceptional results.

By following the recipe in Part 4: Achieve Massive Scale, Worldwide, 24/7 Nonstop, your business is now set up for extreme growth. Watch as your business scales up and sales reach levels you only dreamed of. And remember, it's your passion, your mindset and dedication that will drive you forward. The world is waiting for you to claim your place among successful entrepreneurs.

If I could do this, so can you because it's a tried-and-true method. Success is within your reach – so go out there and make it a reality!

Before I wrap this book up, I want to let you know I'm here to support you in any way that makes sense for your business. At the company I founded, DistroChannels.com, we continuously work hard on streamlining this entire process, and our platform DistroList.app connects you directly to those persons, places, and things that have access to your target buyers so that you can make money fast. So if you're looking for more support, head over to DistroChannels.com. It's not just a website – it's a platform designed to help you achieve the success you want for your business. We've got you covered whether you're a hands-on DIY (Do It Yourself) type, want a bit of guidance with a DWY (Done With You) option, or prefer to sit back while we handle it all with the D4U (Done For You) approach. Regardless of which direction you choose, I hope this book has been insightful, and I wish you the best of success.

We're constantly upgrading and improving our methods for creating powerful distribution networks, so check out the new innovations we've got going on at DistroChannels.com. We're available whenever you need more support.

www.ingramcontent.com/pod-product-compliance
Lightning Source LLC
Chambersburg PA
CBHW030421290526
45786CB00001B/78